MADAMA BUTTERFLY

Opera in Three Acts

Music by

Giacomo Puccini

Libretto by
L. ILLICA and G. GIACOSA

Based on the book by John L. Long
and the drama by David Belasco

English Version
by
JOHN GUTMAN

Ed. 2498

G. SCHIRMER, *Inc.*

Important Notice

Performances of this opera must be licensed by the publisher.

All rights of any kind with respect to this opera and any parts thereof, including but not limited to stage, radio, television, motion picture, mechanical reproduction, translation, printing, and selling are strictly reserved.

License to perform this work, in whole or in part, whether with instrumental or keyboard accompaniment, must be secured in writing from the Publisher. Terms will be quoted upon request.

Copying of either separate parts or the whole of this work, by hand or by any other process, is unlawful and punishable under the provisions of the U.S.A. Copyright Act.

The use of any copies, including arrangements and orchestrations, other than those issued by the Publisher, is forbidden.

All inquiries should be directed to the Publisher:

G. Schirmer Rental Department
5 Bellvale Road
Chester, NY 10918
(914) 469-2271

MADAMA BUTTERFLY

The plot on which *Madama Butterfly* is based first appeared in Century Magazine, 1898, as a short story by the American author, John Luther Long. Through his sister, wife of a missionary stationed in Nagasaki, Long had heard the tale of a Japanese geisha wed to a United States naval officer and then forsaken by him for a bride from his own country. David Belasco, the well-known playwright, director and producer, and a highly individualistic force in the New York theater during the early years of this century, dramatized the story and presented it at the Herald Square Theater on March 5, 1900. The play, starring Blanche Bates as the Japanese girl, was in one act and shared a double bill with Belasco's "Naughty Anthony." It scored a great popular success. The same year, while Puccini was in London to supervise a performance of *Tosca* at Covent Garden, he saw a production of "Madame Butterfly" at the Duke of York's Theatre.

Puccini, though unable to follow the English dialogue, was so moved by the impact of the play that he longed to set it to music at once. Negotiations with Belasco dragged on for more than a year until a contract was signed releasing the operatic rights; and nearly three years followed before the new lyric drama was completed.

On February 17, 1904, when *Madama Butterfly* was booed at its world premiere and the composer took refuge backstage in a dressing room at La Scala so that he might shut out the hostile noise, Puccini stood in full career, with *Manon Lescaut*, *La Bohème* and *Tosca* to his credit. He was the idol of the Italian operatic world, a celebrity whose works were performed on every continent where lyric theaters were available.

On the day following the disastrous premiere, a council of war was held in Puccini's Milan apartment with the composer, the prima donna, the two librettists (Illica and Giacosa) and the publishers in attendance. It was decided to withdraw the opera from performance. Puccini also resolved upon certain revisions for future mountings of *Butterfly*. Within a short time, these revisions were accomplished. Overworked handling of minor characters during the wedding scene of the first act was eliminated. A suave melody for B. F. Pinkerton, the villain-hero, was interpolated in the closing scene (*Addio, fiorito asil*). The lay figure of Kate Pinkerton was cut to a minimum, her finest musical phrase being switched to the heroine, Cio-Cio-San (*Sotto il gran ponte del cielo*). Most important of all, the long second act was divided into Acts Two and Three, the interlude now serving as curtain-raiser, following an intermission, to the final tableau. The quantitative amount of revision was not great — thirty-odd pages in the full orchestral score — but its strategic importance turned out to be overwhelming. On May 28th of the same year as the unsuccessful premiere, *Madama Butterfly* made a second entrance upon the scene in the relatively modest theater of Brescia. Since the original Cio-Cio-San, Rosina Storchio, was by this time fulfilling previous contracts in South America, a new heroine, Salomea Krucenisca, was engaged. Most of musical Milan came to Brescia for the performance; and now, with its masterly revisions pointing up the excellence of the work as a whole, *Butterfly* won a triumph which has never since been reversed.

THE STORY

ACT I. On a flowering terrace above Nagasaki harbor, U.S. Navy Lieutenant B. F. Pinkerton inspects the house he has leased from a marriage broker, Goro, who has procured him three servants and a geisha wife known as Madama Butterfly (Cio-Cio-San). To American Consul Sharpless, who arrives breathless from climbing the hill, Pinkerton describes his carefree philosophy of a navy man roaming the world in search of pleasure. For the moment, he is enchanted with the fragile Cio-Cio-San and intends to go through a marriage ceremony with her —for ninety-nine years, but subject to monthly renewal. When Sharpless warns that the girl may not take her vows so lightly as he regards his, the Lieutenant brushes aside such scruples, adding that he will one day take a "real" American wife. At that moment Cio-Cio-San is heard in the distance joyously singing of her wedding day. After she has entered, surrounded by her friends, she tells Pinkerton how, when her family fell on hard times, she had to earn her living as a geisha. Soon her relatives arrive and noisily express their opinions on the marriage. When she finds a quiet moment, Cio-Cio-San shows her bridegroom her few earthly treasures, telling him her intention of embracing his Christian faith. With much pomp and ceremony the Imperial Commissioner performs the wedding ceremony, after which the guests toast the couple. Suddenly Cio-Cio-San's uncle, a Buddhist priest, bursts upon the scene, cursing the girl for having renounced her ancestors' religion. Pinkerton angrily orders priest and family to leave. Alone with his bride, he dries her tears and reminds her that night is falling. Helped by her maid Suzuki into a pure white kimono, Cio-Cio-San joins the ardent Pinkerton in the moonlit garden, where they sing of their love. Swept on the tides of passion, the lieutenant picks up his tiny bride and carries her into the house.

ACT II. Three years later, Cio-Cio-San still waits for her husband's return. As Suzuki prays to her gods for aid, her mistress stands by the doorway, her eyes fixed on the harbor. The maid urges Cio-Cio-San to remarry, for Pinkerton will never return; in reply, she bids Suzuki have faith—one fine day his ship will appear on the horizon. The Consul comes with a letter from the lieutenant, but before he can read it to Cio-Cio-San, Goro, who has been lurking outside, brings in the latest of a long line of suitors for her hand. The girl dismisses both him and the wealthy Prince Yamadori, insisting that her American husband has not deserted her. When they are alone, Sharpless again starts to read her the letter, suggesting as tactfully as he can that Pinkerton may never return. Cio-Cio-San proudly carries forth their child, insisting that as soon as Pinkerton knows of his son, he will surely come back. Moved by her devotion and lacking the heart to tell her of the lieutenant's remarriage, Sharpless leaves. Cio-Cio-San, on the point of despair, hears a cannon report; seizing a spyglass, she discovers Pinkerton's ship entering the harbor. Delirious with joy, she orders Suzuki to help her strew the house with flower petals. Then, as night falls, she dons her wedding gown and, with her son and Suzuki, waits by the door for her husband's return.

ACT III. As dawns breaks, Suzuki insists that Cio-Cio-San rest. Humming a lullaby to her child, she carries him to another room. Before long, Sharpless, Pinkerton and then Kate, his new wife, enter. When Suzuki realizes who the American woman is, she collapses in despair; out of consideration for her mistress, however, she agrees to aid in breaking the news to her. Pinkerton, overcome with remorse, bids an anguished farwell to the scene of his former happiness, then rushes away. No sooner is he gone than Cio-Cio-San comes forth, expecting to find him but finding Kate instead. She takes but a moment to guess the truth. Leaning on Suzuki for support, she agrees to give up her child if the father will return for him. Then sending even Suzuki away, she takes forth the dagger with which her father committed suicide and bows before a statute of Buddha. Just as she raises the blade, Suzuki pushes the child into the room. Tearfully sobbing a farewell to him, Cio-Cio-San sends him into the garden to play. Then, crouching behind a screen, she stabs herself, falling forward in the agony of death as Pinkerton's voice is heard in the distance calling her name.

Courtesy of Opera News

CAST OF CHARACTERS

MADAMA BUTTERFLY (Cio-Cio-San) . . . . Soprano

SUZUKI, her servant . . . . Mezzo-Soprano

KATE PINKERTON . . . . Mezzo-Soprano

B. F. PINKERTON, Lieutenant in the United States Navy . . . . . Tenor

SHARPLESS, United States Consul at Nagasaki . . . Baritone

GORO, a marriage broker . . . . Tenor

PRINCE YAMADORI . . . . Baritone

THE BONZE, Cio-Cio-San's uncle . . . . Bass

YAKUSIDÉ . . . . Baritone

THE IMPERIAL COMMISSIONER . . . . Bass

THE OFFICIAL REGISTRAR . . . . Baritone

CIO-CIO-SAN'S MOTHER . . . . Mezzo-Soprano

THE AUNT . . . . Mezzo-Soprano

THE COUSIN . . . . Soprano

TROUBLE, Cio-Cio-San's child

Cio-Cio-San's relatives and friends, servants

The action takes place at Nagasaki.

MADAMA BUTTERFLY

ATTO PRIMO

COLINA PRESSO NAGASAKI

Casa giapponese, terrazza e giardino. In
fondo, al basso, la rada, il porto, la
città di Nagasaki.

PINKERTON E GORO

(*Goro fa visitare la casa a Pinkerton,
che passa di sorpresa in sorpresa.*)

PINKERTON

E soffitto ... e pareti ...

GORO
(*godendo della sorprese*)

Vanno e vengono a prova
a norma che vi giova
nello stesso locale
alternar nuovi aspetti ai consueti.

PINKERTON
(*cercando intorno*)

Il nido nuzïal
dov'è?

GORO
(*accennando a due locali*)

Qui, o là ... secondo ...

PINKERTON

Anch'esso a doppio fondo!
La sala?

GORO
(*mostra la terrazza*)

Ecco!

PINKERTON
(*stupito*)

All'aperto?...

GORO
(*mostrando il chiudersi d'una parete*)

Un fianco scorre ...

PINKERTON

Capisco! Un altro ...

GORO

Scivola!

PINKERTON

E la dimora frivola ...

GORO
(*protestando*)

Salda come una torre
da terra, fino al tetto.

PINKERTON

È una casa a soffietto.

GORO

(*batte tre volte le mani palma a palma;
entrano due uomini ed una donna e
si genuflettono innanzi a Pinkerton*)

Questa è la cameriera

(*accennando*)

che della vostra sposa
fu già serva amorosa.
Il cuoco ... il servitor. Son confusi
del grande onore.

PINKERTON

I nomi?

GORO
(*presentando*)

Miss Nuvola leggiera —
Raggio di sol nascente. — Esala aromi.

SUZUKI
(*fatta ardita*)

Sorride Vostro Onore? —
Il riso è frutto e fiore.
Disse il savio Ocunama:
dei crucci la trama
smaglia il sorriso. Schiude alla perla il
     guscio,
apre all'uom l'uscio
del Paradiso.
Profumo degli Dei ...
Fontana della vita ...

(*Goro accorgendosi che Pinkerton comincia ad essere infastidito dalla lo-
quela di Suzuki batte le mani. — I
tre si alzano e fuggono rapidamente
rientrando in casa*).

PINKERTON

A chiacchiere costei
mi par cosmopolita.

(*a Goro andato in fondo ad osservare*)

Che guardi?

GORO

Se non giunge ancor la sposa.

PINKERTON

Tutto è pronto?

MADAMA BUTTERFLY

ACT I

(*From the room at the rear of the little house Goro, bowing repeatedly, shows in Pinkerton and pompously, although servilely, points out the little house in detail.*)

PINKERTON

Both the walls and the ceilings . . .

GORO
(*enjoying Pinkerton's surprise*)
can be easily shifted
and, if you want it lifted,
every part of this building
can be changed
to adjust to changing feelings.

PINKERTON
(*looking around*)
I wonder where the bed might be?

GORO
(*He points to two places.*)
It's where you put it.

PINKERTON

That's what I call ingenious!
The living room?

GORO
(*showing the terrace*)
Here, Sir.

PINKERTON
(*astonished*)
In the open?

GORO
(*slides the wall towards the terrace*)
Just slide this wall back.

PINKERTON

I get it! It's stunning! And this one . . .

GORO

Movable!

PINKERTON

Seems rather like a house of cards.

GORO
(*protesting*)
Strong as an ancient fortress, from cellar to the ceiling.

PINKERTON

We'll find out when the wind blows.

(*Goro claps his hands three times. Two men and a woman enter and humbly genuflect on the terrace in front of Pinkerton.*)

GORO
(*pointing*)
This one will be your housemaid:
she's been a faithful servant
to your lovely intended.
The cook . . . and here's the house-boy.
They're confused: this is too much honor.

PINKERTON

Their names, please?

GORO

She's called Miss Cloud from Heaven.
Ray of the Sun that's rising.
Breath of Aroma.

SUZUKI

I see Your Honor's smiling?
A smile is like a flower.
Says the wise Ocunama:
A smile will unravel the skein of your sorrow.
Smiles free the pearls from the oyster,
open to a man all the gates of Heaven,
The perfume of the Godhead and Life's eternal fountain.
Says the wise Ocunama:
A smile will unravel the skein of your sorrow.

(*Noticing that Pinkerton is becoming annoyed at Suzuki's chatter he claps his hands three times. The three rise and leave quickly, re-entering the house.*)

PINKERTON

It's everywhere the same: they babble on like parrots!

(*to Goro, who has gone to the rear to look out*)
No news yet?

GORO

No, the bride has not arrived yet.

PINKERTON

All is ready?

1

GORO

Ogni cosa.

PINKERTON

Gran perla di sensale!

GORO

(*ringrazia con profondo inchino*)

Qui verran: l'Ufficiale
del registro, i parenti, il vostro Console,
la fidanzata. Qui si firma l'atto
e il matrimonio è fatto.

PINKERTON

E son molti i parenti?

GORO

La suocera, la nonna, lo zio Bonzo
(che non ci degnerà di sua presenza)
e cugini! e le cugine...
Mettiam fra gli ascendenti
ed i collaterali, un due dozzine.
Quanto alla discendenza...

(*con malizia ossequiosa*)

provvederanno assai
Vostra Grazia e la bella Butterfly.

(*si ode la voce di Sharpless il Console,
che sale il colle*)

PINKERTON

Gran perla di sensale!

LA VOCE DI SHARPLESS
(*un po' lontano*)

E suda e arrampica!
sbuffa, inciampica!

GORO

(*che è accorso al fondo, annuncia a
Pinkerton*)

Il Consol sale.

SHARPLESS

(*appare sbuffando: Goro si prosterna
innanzi al Console*)

Ah!...quei ciottoli
m'hanno sfiaccato!

PINKERTON

(*va incontro a Sharpless — i due si
stringono la mano*)

Bene arrivato.

GORO

Bene arrivato.

SHARPLESS

Ouff!

PINKERTON

Presto, Goro,
qualche ristoro.

(*Goro entra in casa frettoloso*)

SHARPLESS

(*guardando intorno*)

Alto.

PINKERTON

(*mostrandogli il panorama*)

Ma bello!

SHARPLESS

(*contemplando il mare e la città sotto-
posti*)

Nagasaki, il mare!
il porto...

PINKERTON

(*accennando alla casa*)

e una casetta
che obbedisce a bacchetta.

SHARPLESS

Vostra?

PINKERTON

La comperai
per novecento novantanove anni,
con facoltà, ogni mese,
di rescindere i patti.
Sono in questo paese
elastici del par case e contratti.

SHARPLESS

E l'uomo esperto ne profitta.

(*Goro viene frettoloso dalla casa, seguito dai due servi; portano bicchieri,
bottiglie e due poltrone di vimini; de-
pongono bicchieri e bottiglie su di un
piccolo tavolo e tornano in casa*)

PINKERTON

Certo.
Dovunque al mondo
lo Yankee vagabondo
si gode e traffica
sprezzando i rischi.
Affonda l'áncora alla ventura
finchè una raffica...

(*Pinkerton's interrompe per offrire da
bere a Sharpless*)

Milk-Punch, o Wisky?

(*riprende*)

...scompigli nave e ormeggi, albera-
tura.
La vita ei non appaga
se non fa suo tesor
i fiori d'ogni plaga,
d'ogni bella gli amor.

GORO
Every detail.
(*thanks him with a deep bow*)

PINKERTON
You are the perfect broker!

GORO
You will see: first the Registrar on
    duty,
all her kinsfolk, your Consul General,
and then your promised.
You will sign a paper,
and that is all there's to it.

PINKERTON
Are the relatives many?

GORO
Her mother and her grandma, Uncle
    Bonzo.
(The latter will not condescend to join
    us.)
Then the cousins, male and female.
Let's say, between ascendants
and quite a few collaterals, about two
    dozen.
But as regards descendants...
    (*with sly servility*)
they will be taken care of
by yourself and the lovely Butterfly.

SHARPLESS
(*off-stage*)
But I'm not a mountaineer!
I never climbed so high!

GORO
(*from the rear, announces to Pinkerton*)
There is your consul.
(*prostrates himself in front of the Con-
    sul*)

SHARPLESS
(*enters, panting*)
Ah! that gravel path,
I just barely made it.

PINKERTON
(*goes up to the Consul; the two
    shake hands.*)
I'm glad to see you.

SHARPLESS
Ouff!

PINKERTON
Hurry, Goro,
bring some refreshments.
(*Goro hastily enters the house.*)

SHARPLESS
(*still breathless, looking around*)
Too high!

PINKERTON
(*pointing to the panorama*)
But pretty!

SHARPLESS
(*looking at the city and the sea below*)
Nagasaki, the ocean,
the harbor...

PINKERTON
(*points to the house*)
...and then this house here:
it's a sorcerer's dream-house.
(*Goro comes hurriedly from the house,
    followed by the two servants; they
    carry glasses and bottles, which they
    place on the terrace; the two serv-
    ants go back into the house while
    Goro prepares the drinks.*)

SHARPLESS
Your house?

PINKERTON
Yes, I have purchased it
for nine hundred ninety-nine long years,
but I can cancel the contract any month.
It's fantastic!
It appears in this country
both houses and agreements are elastic.

SHARPLESS
And if you're smart you take advantage.

PINKERTON
Surely.
(*Pinkerton and Sharpless sit on the
    terrace where Goro has put the drinks.*)
Wherever ships sail you'll find a Yankee
    roaming;
cheerful and unafraid he courts adven-
    ture.
He throws his anchor out
just when and where he chooses.
(*interrupts himself to offer Sharpless a
    drink*)
You'll have some whiskey?
(*starting again*)
He throws his anchor out
just when and where he chooses,
until one day a storm destroys his ship,
and yet he never loses.
To make his life worth living
he must pluck and possess the flowers
    of each region...

SHARPLESS

È un facile vangelo
che fa la vita vaga
ma che intristisce il cuor.

PINKERTON

(continuando)

Vinto si tuffa e la sorte riacciuffa.
Il suo talento
fa in ogni dove.
Così mi sposo all'uso giapponese
per novecento
novantanove anni,
Salvo a prosciogliermi ogni mese.
"America forever!"

SHARPLESS

"America forever." Ed è bella
la sposa?

GORO

(che ha udito, si avanza premuroso ed
insinuante)

Una ghirlanda
di fior freschi. Una stella
dai raggi d'oro.
E per nulla: sol cento yen.

(al Console)

Se Vostra Grazia mi comanda
ce n'ho un assortimento.

(il Console ridendo, ringrazia)

PINKERTON

(con viva impazienza)

Va, conducila Goro.

(Goro corre in fondo e scompare di-
scendendo il colle: i due servi rientrano in casa. Pinkerton e Sharpless
siedono).

SHARPLESS

Quale smania vi prende!
Sareste addirittura cotto?

PINKERTON

Non so!
Dipende dal grado di cottura!
Amore o grillo dir non saprei.

Certo costei
m'ha coll' ingenue arti invescato.
Lieve qual tenue vetro soffiato
alla statura, al portamento
sembra figura da paravento.
Ma dal suo lucido fondo di lacca
come con subito moto si stacca,
qual farfalletta svolazza e posa
con tal grazietta silenziosa
che di rincorrerla furor m'assale
se pure infrangerne dovessi l'ale.

SHARPLESS

(seriamente e bonario)

Ier l'altro, il Consolato
sen' venne a visitar!
Io non la vidi, ma l'udii parlar.
Di sua voce il mistero
l'anima mi colpì.
Certo quando è sincero
l'amor parla così.
Sarebbe gran peccato
le lievi ali strappar
e desolar forse un credulo cuor.
Quella divina
mite vocina
non dovrebbe dar note di dolor.

PINKERTON

Console mio garbato,
quetatevi! Si sa,
la vostra età è di flebile umor.
Non c'è gran male
s'io vo' quell'ale
drizzare ai dolci voli dell'amor!

(offre di nuovo da bere)

Wisky?

SHARPLESS

Un altro bicchiere.

(Pinkerton colma anche il proprio bicchiere)

Bevo alla vostra famiglia lontana.

SHARPLESS

That's a gay and easy credo . . .

PINKERTON

(continuing)

have a girl in every port!

SHARPLESS

You eat your cake and have it!
Your pleasures will be legion,
but what sadness in your heart.

PINKERTON

Always undaunted,
his luck will not desert him.
As long as pleasures last
what is there to hurt him?
And now, according to the local custom,
I shall be married
for nine hundred ninety-nine years.
But it is agreed that I may cancel!

SHARPLESS

A gay and easy credo.

PINKERTON

"The Stars and Stripes forever!"

SHARPLESS

"The Stars and Stripes forever!"
And the bride is a beauty?
(Goro who has listened, appears on the
terrace urgently trying to make his
point.)

GORO

She is a garland of virgin flowers,
like a star with rays that are golden.
Inexpensive: one hundred yen.
(to the Consul)
Suppose Your Honor could be tempted?
I have a nice collection.
(The Consul laughs, thanks him and
gets up.) PINKERTON

Go and see if she's coming.
(Goro runs to the rear and disappears
down the hill.)

SHARPLESS

I can see you're impatient!
Don't tell me that you really love her?

PINKERTON

Who knows? Who knows?
Depending on what you mean by
"loving."
It may be love or it may be a fancy,
but for the moment

I am enthralled
by that innocent charmer:
Light, like a glass-figure spun by a
master
and, in her gestures, gracious and
tender,
she's like the maiden seen on a silk
screen.
But she won't stay in the screen-maker's
power,
and taking wing she alights on a flower:
a butterfly, she escapes me and taunts
me,
in all my dreams so enchants me and
haunts me
that I must give her chase.
I must possess her,
and even though her lovely wings be
broken.

SHARPLESS

(seriously and affably)

Your little girl appeared at my office
not long ago.
I did not see her but I heard her talk.
And the sound of her voice impressed
me,
I don't know why.
Surely, only a love that's true
has such a voice.
I think it would be too bad
to break those tender young wings
and to play games
with a girl's trusting heart.

PINKERTON

Consul, you're a kind man,
don't get upset!
I know
Men of your age have a sentimental
heart.
There'll be no harm done,
if I have my way
and teach those tender wings the flights
of love. SHARPLESS

I hope you'll think it over.
Voices like her voice
should sing a love-song,
never speak of unhappiness in love.

PINKERTON

(again offering him a drink)

Whiskey? SHARPLESS

I don't mind another.
(Pinkerton pours whiskey for Sharpless
and fills his own glass.)
(raising his glass) Here is a toast to
your folks back in Kansas.

PINKERTON
(*leva il calice*)

E al giorno in cui mi sposerò con vere
nozze, a una vera sposa americana.

GORO

(*riappare correndo, venendo dal basso
della collina*)

Ecco! Son giunte al sommo del pendìo.
          (*accennando verso il sentiero*)

Già del femmineo sciame
qual di vento in fogliame
s'ode il brusìo.

LE AMICHE

Ah!
Quanto cielo! Quanto mar!

VOCE DI BUTTERFLY

Ancora un passo or via. Aspetta.

ALTRE VOCI

Come sei tarda.
Ecco la vetta.
Guarda, guarda quanti fior!

VOCE DI BUTTERFLY

Spira sul mare e sulla terra
un primaveril soffio giocondo.
Io sono la fanciulla
più lieta del Giappone, anzi del mondo.
Amiche, io son venuta
al richiamo d'amor;
d'amor venni alle soglie
ove s'accoglie
il bene di chi vive e di chi muor.

LE AMICHE

Gioia a te sia
dolce amica, ma pria
di varcare la soglia che t' attira
volgiti e mira
le cose tutte che ti son sì care.
Quanti fior! Quanto cielo! Quanto
     mare!

SHARPLESS

O allegro cinguettar di gioventù!

(*Appaiono, superato il pendìo della
collina, Butterfly colle amiche, tutte
hanno grandi ombrelli aperti, a vivi
colori*)

BUTTERFLY
Siam giunte.
(*vede il gruppo dei tre uomini e rico-
nosce Pinkerton. Chiude subito l'om-
brello e pronta addita Pinkerton alle
amiche*)
B. F. Pinkerton. Giù.
          (*si genuflette*)
LE AMICHE
(*chiudono gli ombrelli e si genufletto-
no*)
Giù.
(*poi tutte si alzano e si avvicinano a
Pinkerton, cerimoniosamente*)
BUTTERFLY
Gran ventura.
LE AMICHE
Riverenza.
PINKERTON
(*sorridendo*)
È un po' dura
la scalata?
BUTTERFLY
(*compassata*)
A una sposa
costumata
più penosa è
l' impazienza. . .
PINKERTON
(*un po' derisorio*)
Molto raro
complimento.
BUTTERFLY
(*ingenua*)
Dei più belli
ancor ne so.
PINKERTON
(*rincalzando*)
Dei gioielli!
BUTTERFLY
(*volendo sfoggiare il suo repertorio di
complimenti*)
Se vi è caro
sul momento . . .
PINKERTON
Grazie . . . no.
SHARPLESS
(*ha osservato prima curiosamente il
gruppo delle fanciulle, poi si è avvi-
cinato a Butterfly che lo ascolta con
attenzione*)
Miss Butterfly. Bel nome, vi sta a meraviglia.
Siete di Nagasaki?
BUTTERFLY
Signor sì. Di famiglia
assai prospera un tempo.
          (*alle amiche*)
Verità?

PINKERTON
(*also raising his glass*)
And also to the happy day
when I shall marry
one of the pretty girls of the good old
U.S.A.

GORO
(*reappears running breathlessly from
the foot of the hill*)
See them?
They're coming, they're coming up the
hill!
(*pointing toward the path*)
And all the girls around her,
how they chatter like the wind
that sings in the tree-tops.

THE GIRLS
Ah! all this heaven! all this sea!

BUTTERFLY
We almost have arrived.

THE GIRLS
You are the last one.

BUTTERFLY
I'm coming.

THE GIRLS
We're on the hilltop.
All these flowers! All this light!

BUTTERFLY
(*serenely*)
Above the ocean
in the tree-tops,
once again we feel the breeze of springtime!
No girl in all Japan
can be happier than I am,
nor in the whole world.
Remember why I came here:
It was love that had called,
and love is here to greet me.

THE GIRLS
Lift up your glances and see
the things you have treasured:
All this radiant heaven! all this sea!
All these flowers! All this light!
Happy girl,
may you be always so happy!

SHARPLESS
How sweet this cheerful chatter of
young girls!

BUTTERFLY
I see him.
(*sees the three men, and recognizes
Pinkerton; immediately closes her
umbrella and points him out to her
friends*)
B. F. Pinkerton. Bow!
(*She genuflects.*)

THE GIRLS
(*closing their umbrellas and genuflect-
ing*)
Bow.
(*They all rise and approach Pinkerton
ceremoniously.*)

BUTTERFLY
I'm delighted.

THE GIRLS
We are honored.

PINKERTON
(*smiling*)
Did you find the climbing trying?

BUTTERFLY
For a girl who meets her husband much
more trying is the waiting.

PINKERTON
(*kindly but with a little derision*)
That's a compliment I treasure.

BUTTERFLY
(*naively*)
I could tell you many more.

PINKERTON
(*as before, only more so*)
Purest jewels!

BUTTERFLY
(*wishing to brag with her store of com-
pliments*)
Shall I tell them for your pleasure?

PINKERTON
Thank you: no.

SHARPLESS
(*First he curiously looks at the group of
girls, then he draws near Butterfly,
who listens attentively to him.*)
Miss Butterfly. A sweet name,
and also so fitting.
Are you from Nagasaki?

BUTTERFLY
Yes, I am.
And my family was rather wealthy.
(*to her friends*) Is it true?

LE AMICHE
(*approvando premurose*)
Verità!

BUTTERFLY
Nessuno si confessa mai nato in povertà
e non c'è vagabondo che a sentirlo non
sia di gran prosapia. Eppure
conobbi la ricchezza. Ma il turbine
rovescia
le quercie più robuste ... e abbiam fatto la ghescia
per sostentarci.
(*alle amiche*)
Vero?

LE AMICHE
(*confermano*)
Vero!

BUTTERFLY
Non lo nascondo
nè m' adonto.
(*vedendo che Sharpless sorride*)
Ridete? Perchè? ... Cose del mondo.

PINKERTON
(*ha ascoltato con interesse e si rivolge a
Sharpless*)
(Con quel fare di bambola quando parla m'infiamma.)

SHARPLESS
(*anch'esso interessato dalle chiacchiere
di Butterfly, continua a interrogarla*)
E ci avete sorelle?

BUTTERFLY
No signore. Ho la mamma.

GORO
(*con importanza*)
Una nobile dama.

BUTTERFLY
Ma senza farle torto
povera molto anch'essa.

SHARPLESS
E vostro padre?

BUTTERFLY
(*si arresta sorpresa — poi secco secco
risponde:*)
Morto.

SHARPLESS
(*a Butterfly*)
Quanti anni avete?

BUTTERFLY
(*con civetteria quasi infantile*)
Indovinate.

PINKERTON
Dieci.

BUTTERFLY
Crescete.

SHARPLESS
Venti.

BUTTERFLY
Calate.
Quindici, netti, netti;
sono vecchia diggià.

SHARPLESS
Quindici anni!

PINKERTON
Quindici anni!

SHARPLESS
L'età dei giuochi ...

PINKERTON
e dei confetti
(*Goro nel seguire i servi che rientrano
in casa si accorge che altre persone
salgono il colle: osserva; poi corre ad
annunciare a Pinkerton e a Sharpless:*)

GORO
(*con importanza*)
L'imperial Commissario e l'Ufficiale
del registro — i congiunti.

PINKERTON
(*a Goro*)
Fate presto.
(*Goro corre in casa*)
Che burletta
la sfilata
della nova parentela,
tolta imprestito a mesata.

ALCUNI PARENTI
(*con molta curiosità a Butterfly*)
Dov'è? dov'è?

BUTTERFLY
(*indicando Pinkerton*)
Eccolo là!

I.a CUGINA
Bello non è.

BUTTERFLY
(*offesa*)
Bello è così
che non si può
sognar di più.

THE GIRLS
(*eagerly agreeing*)
That is true.

BUTTERFLY
I know that no one will admit
his family was poor,
and the humblest vagabond will say
he was born of noble forebears.
The fact remains that we were wealthy
    once.
But when storms begin to rage
even strongest oaks will tumble.
We had to work as geishas
to keep the wolf away.
(*to her friends*) Did we?

THE GIRLS
(*they agree*)
Always!

BUTTERFLY
I do not hide it, and why should I?
(*seeing that Sharpless is laughing*)
You're laughing? But why?
That's how the world goes.

PINKERTON
(*has listened with interest and turns to
    Sharpless*)
(When she talks like a grown-up child,
I can't help but adore her.)

SHARPLESS
(*also interested in Butterfly's chatter,
    continues to question her*)

SHARPLESS
Do you have any sisters?

BUTTERFLY
No, no sisters. But a mother.

GORO
(*importantly*)
A most honorable lady.

BUTTERFLY
But if you want the whole truth,
She is a poor as I am.

SHARPLESS
And where's your father?

BUTTERFLY
(*is taken by surprise, then replies
    dryly*):
Dead.

SHARPLESS
And how old are you?

BUTTERFLY
(*with almost childlike coquetry*)
Why don't you guess it.

SHARPLESS
Ten years.

BUTTERFLY
Too little.

SHARPLESS
Twenty.

BUTTERFLY
Too much.
I am exactly fifteen.
I'm afraid I'm quite old.

SHARPLESS
She is fifteen!

PINKERTON
That's a nice age!

SHARPLESS
An age for playing . . .

PINKERTON
and merry pastimes.

GORO
(*who has noticed other people arriv-
    ing from the rear, announces im-
    portantly*):
The Imperial official,
and the Registrar on duty,
and the kinsfolk.

PINKERTON
(*to Goro*)
Go and hurry.
(*Goro runs into the house.*)

PINKERTON
Very funny!
All these in-laws are a recent acqui-
    sition
hired on a monthly basis.

RELATIVES AND GIRLFRIENDS
(*to Butterfly*)
Where's he?

BUTTERFLY
(*pointing to Pinkerton*)
Right over there.

COUSIN
Handsome he's not.

BUTTERFLY
(*offended*)
He is a prince.
Even in dreams they're hard to find.

LA MADRE DI BUTTERFLY
Mi pare un re!

LO ZIO
Vale un Perù.

PINKERTON
Certo dietro a quella vela
di ventaglio pavonazzo
la mia suocera si cela.
E quel coso da strapazzo
è lo zio briaco e pazzo.

I.A CUGINA
Goro l'offrì
pur anche a me.
Ma s'ebbe un no!

BUTTERFLY (sdegnosa)
Sì, giusto tu!

ALCUNI AMICI AD ALCUNE AMICHE
Ecco, perchè
prescelta fu,
vuol far con te
la soprappiù.

ALTRE AMICHE
La sua beltà
gia disfiorì.

CUGINI E CUGINE
Divorzierà.

ALTRI
Spero di sì.

GORO
Per carità
tacete un po'...
chi v'insegnò
la civiltà?

LA MADRE DI BUTTERFLY E ALCUNE
CUGINE
Oh quella lì
non smette più

GORO
Stoltezza fu
condurla qui.

LO ZIO
Vino ce n'è?

LE MADRE E LA ZIA
Guardiamo un po'.

ALCUNE AMICHE
Ne vidi già
color di thè,

GORO
e chèrmisì!
Per carità tacete un po'... Sch! sch!

SHARPLESS
O amico fortunato!
O fortunato Pinkerton,
che in sorte v'è toccato
un fior pur or sbocciato!
Non più bella e d'assai
fanciulla io vidi mai di questa
   Butterfly.
E se a voi sembran scede
il patto e la sua fede.
Badate! Ella ci crede.

PINKERTON
Sì,è vero,è un fiore!
L'esotico suo odore
m'ha il cervello sconvolto.
E in fede mia l'ho colto!

BUTTERFLY
(a sua madre)
Mamma, vien qua.
(agli altri)
Badate a me:
attenti, orsù,
uno — due — tre
e tutti giù.
(e tutti si inchinano innanzi a Pinkerton,
   tranne il Commissario e l'Ufficiale)
(Intanto Goro ha fatto portare dai
   servi alcuni tavolini, sui quali dispon-
   gonsi varie confetture, pasticcietti, li-
   quori, vini e servizi da thè; si portano alcuni cuscini e un tavolino a
   parte, coll' occorrente per scrivere.
   Parenti, amici guardano con molta
   soddisfazione i dolciumi portati. Butterfly presenta i parenti a Pinkerton).

PINKERTON
Vieni amor mio!
Ti piace la casetta?

BUTTERFLY
(alzandosi)
Signor B. F. Pinkerton, perdono...
(mostra le mani e la braccia che sono
   impacciate dalle maniche rigonfie)
io vorrei... pochi oggetti
da donna...

PINKERTON
Dove sono?

BUTTERFLY
(indicando le maniche)
Sono qui — vi dispiace?

PINKERTON
(un po' sorpreso, sorride... poi subito
   acconsente, con galanteria)
O perchè mai,
mia bella Butterfly!?

BUTTERFLY
(a mano a mano cava dalle maniche gli
   oggetti e li depone sopra uno sgabello)
Fazzoletti.— La pipa.— Una cintura.—
Un piccolo fermaglio.—
Uno specchio.— Un ventaglio.

PINKERTON
(vede un vasetto)
Quel barattolo?

MOTHER

I think he's great.

UNCLE
(pointing to Pinkerton)

Handsome and tall.

PINKERTON

Look: behind this purple fan there
is a lady, shy and shrinking.
That's my mother-in-law, I'll wager.
And this old, decrepit codger
is an uncle who likes drinking.

A FEMALE COUSIN

First Goro offered him to me.

BUTTERFLY
(disdainfully)

Don't make me laugh!

CHORUS
(to the cousins)

And just because it's her he chose
she thinks she can turn up her nose.

OTHERS

She's not as pretty as she was.

COUSINS

She'll be divorced.

COUSIN

I hope she will.

GORO

For heaven's sake,
can't you be still!

YAKUSIDE

Is there no wine?

MOTHER AND AUNT

Let's have a look.

CHORUS

I've seen the wine . . .
as brown as tea,
a very lovely sight to see!

GORO

For heaven's sake, can't you be still?
Sh! sh! sh!

SHARPLESS

You are a lucky devil!
I'll call you "Lucky Pinkerton!"
What else but luck has sent you
that pure and fragrant flower!
I must say I've not seen yet seen
a girl as lovely as your pretty Butterfly.
Though you waste no emotion
on this marriage and on her devotion,
I warn you! she is in earnest. (points
to Butterfly)

PINKERTON

It's true she is a flower!
So strange, so strongly scented
that my head whirls with her fragrance.
A flower so pure and tender,
to own her will be delightful!

BUTTERFLY
(to her relatives)

Now listen, please, to me.
Mother, come here.
(to the others)
Listen to me: do as I say.
One, two, three, everyone down.
(At a signal from Butterfly, they all bow
to Pinkerton and Sharpless.)

PINKERTON

(The relatives disperse into the garden; Goro takes some of them into
the house. Pinkerton takes Butterfly
by the hand and leads her toward
the house.)
Come here, my darling!
How do you like your new house?

BUTTERFLY

Now, Mister B. F. Pinkerton, allow me
. . . (shows her hands and arms
which are covered by flowing
sleeves)
I would like to show you some of
my own things.

PINKERTON

And where are they?

BUTTERFLY
(pointing to the sleeves)

They're right here . . . do you mind?

PINKERTON

(slightly surprised, smiles; then suddenly acquiesces with great courtesy)
Why should I mind, my pretty Butterfly?

BUTTERFLY

(One by one she takes various objects
from her sleeves and gives them to
Suzuki, who has come out on the terrace and puts them in the house.)
Silken kerchiefs. A pipe.
Here is a belt, and here a little buckle,
and a mirror, and a fan.

PINKERTON
(seeing a little jar)

What might this one be?

BUTTERFLY

Un vaso di tintura.

PINKERTON

Ohibò!

BUTTERFLY

Vi spiace? . . .

(lo getta)

Via!

(trae un astuccio lungo a stretto)

PINKERTON

E quello?

BUTTERFLY

(molto seria)

Cosa sacra e mia.

PINKERTON

E non si può vedere?

BUTTERFLY

(supplichevole e grave)

C'è troppa gente.
Perdonate.

(depone l'astuccio con gran rispetto)

GORO

*(intanta si è avvicinato e dice all'orec-
chio di Pinkerton)*

È un presente
del Mikado a suo padre . . coll'invito . .

(fa il gesto di chi s'apre il ventre)

PINKERTON

(piano a Goro)

E . . . suo padre?

GORO

Ha obbedito.

*(s' allontana, mescolandosi agli
invitati)*

BUTTERFLY

*(leva dalle maniche alcune statuette e
le mostra a Pinkerton)*

Gli Ottokè.

PINKERTON

*(ne prende una e la esamina con
curiosità)*

Quei pupazzi? . . . Avete detto?

BUTTERFLY

Son l'anime degli avi.

PINKERTON

Ah! . . . il mio rispetto.

(depone la statuetta presso le altre)

BUTTERFLY

*(trae Pinkerton in disparte e con tenera
e rispettosa confidenza gli dice:)*

Ieri sono salita
tutta sola in secreto alla Missione.
Colla nuova mia vita
posso adottare nuova religione.
Lo zio Bonzo nol sa,
nè i miei lo sanno. Io seguo il mio
destino
e piena d'umiltà
al Dio del signor Pinkerton m'inchino.
È mio destino. Nella stessa chiesetta
in ginocchio con voi pregherò
lo stesso Dio.
E per farvi contento
potrò forse obliar la gente mia.
Amore mio!

*(va a prendere le statuette, le nasconde.
Intanto Goro si è avvicinato al Console, e ricevutone gli ordini, grida
con voce tonante da banditore:)*

GORO

Tutti zitti!

*(cessano le chiacchiere: tutti tralasci-
ano di mangiare e di bere e si avan-
zano in circolo ascoltando con grande
raccoglimento: Pinkerton e Butterfly
stanno nel mezzo)*

IL COMMISSARIO IMPERIALE

(legge)

È concesso al nominato
Benjamin Franklin Pinkerton,
Luogotenente nella cannoniera
Lincoln, marina degli Stati Uniti
America del Nord:
ed alla damigella Butterfly,
del quartiere di Omara-Nagasaki,
d'unirsi in matrimonio, per diritto
il primo della propria voluntà,
. . . ed ella per consenso dei parenti
qui testimoni all'atto.

(porge l'atto per la firma)

GORO

(cerimonioso)

Lo sposo.

(Pinkerton firma)

Poi la sposa.

(Butterfly firma)

BUTTERFLY

A bottle full of dye-stuff.

PINKERTON

Good Lord!

BUTTERFLY

Don't like it?

(*throws away the rouge jar*)

There!

(*She holds up a long narrow box.*)

PINKERTON

And this one?

BUTTERFLY

(*very seriously*)

That is something sacred.

PINKERTON

I'm not allowed to see it?

BUTTERFLY

Too many people. Please excuse me.

(*disappears into the house carrying the box with her*)

GORO

(*who has come near, whispers to Pinkerton*)

That's a gift from our Mikado to her father

with the order ...

(*makes a gesture indicating* hara-kiri)

PINKERTON

(*softly to Goro*)

And her father?

GORO

... followed orders.

(*goes away, and re-enters the house*)

BUTTERFLY

(*Butterfly, who has returned, goes to sit on the terrace near Pinkerton, and takes some small statues from her sleeves.*)

The *Ottoke.*

PINKERTON

(*takes one and examines it curiously*)

... What, those puppets? What did you call them?

BUTTERFLY

The spirits of my forebears.

(*putting down the statues*)

PINKERTON

Ah! I pay them homage.

BUTTERFLY

(*to Pinkerton, in confidence, but respectfully*)

No one is to know it,

I have been on a visit to the Mission.

Starting out in a new life,

I feel I should adopt a new religion.

Uncle Bonzo doesn't know, and my folks don't know it.

But I must heed the call of Fate.

In all humility

I'll bow to Mister Pinkerton's Almighty.

Fate bids me do it.

In the church where you worship

I shall fall on my knees,

and your Lord shall then be my Lord.

And to show how I love you,

I would even abandon my own people.

(*throws herself into Pinkerton's arms*)

That's how I love you! (*She stops as though her relatives might overhear her.*)

GORO

Silence! silence!

(*Meanwhile, Goro has opened the* shosi. *In the room where everything is ready for the wedding, Sharpless and the authorities wait. Butterfly enters and kneels; Pinkerton is standing near her; the relatives are in the garden; they turn toward the house, kneeling.*)

THE COMMISSARY

(*reading*)

It is granted to those here present:

Benjamin Franklin Pinkerton,

a First Lieutenant serving on the gunboat *Lincoln,*

a ship of the United States of North America:

and, on the other side, Miss Butterfly,

who resides in Omara Nagasaki,

to enter holy wedlock.

The first-named party

by his wish and own free will,

the second by consent of all her kinsmen,

witnessing these proceedings.

(*offering the scroll for signature*)

GORO

(*very ceremoniously*)

The husband.

(*Pinkerton signs.*)

Now the bride.

(*Butterfly signs.*)

E tutto è fatto
(*circondano Butterfly festeggiandola*)

LE AMICHE

Madama Butterfly!

BUTTERFLY
(*le corregge*)

Madama B. F. Pinkerton.

(*L'Ufficiale dello Stato Civile ritira l'atto e avverte il Commissario che tutto è finito.*)

IL COMMISSARIO IMPERIALE
(*congedandosi da Pinkerton*)

Auguri molti.

PINKERTON

I miei ringraziamenti.

IL COMMISSARIO IMPERIALE
(*al Console*)

Il signor Console scende?

SHARPLESS

L'accompagno. Ci vedrem domani.

PINKERTON

A meraviglia.

UFFICIALE

(*congedandosi da Pinkerton*)

Posterità.

PINKERTON

Mi proverò.

SHARPLESS
(*stringendo la mano a Pinkerton*)

Giudizio!

(*Pinkerton accompagna i tre sino al sentiero che scende alla città e li saluta di nuovo quando già sono fuori di vista; sono passati prima fra due schiere di parenti e di amiche che li hanno salutati con molti cerimoniosi inchini. Butterfly si è recata presso sua madre. Pinkerton ritorna, e si capisce che è deliberato di sbarazzarsi dei parenti e delle amiche*).

(Ed eccoci in famiglia.
Sbrighiamoci al più presto in modo onesto.)
Hip! hip!

TUTTI (*brindando*)

O Kami! O Kami!

PINKERTON

Beviamo ai novissimi legami.

TUTTI

O Kami! O Kami!

(*Grida terribili dal sentiero della collina interrompono i brindisi: ad un tratto appare dal fondo uno strano personaggio, la cui vista fa allibire tutti. È il Bonzo che si fa innanzi furibondo e, vista Butterfly, stende le mani minacciose verso di lei, gridando*)

IL BONZO

Cio-cio-san! . . . Cio-cio-san! . . .
Abbominazione!

GORO

(*infastidito dalla venuta del Bonzo*)

Un corno al guastafeste!
Chi ci leva d'intorno
le persone moleste?! . . .

(*fa cenno ai servi di asportare tavolini, sgabelli, cuscini e prudentemente se ne parte adiratissimo, borbottando*)

TUTTI

(*impauriti, si raccolgono in un angolo balbettando*)

Lo zio Bonzo!

(*Pinkerton guarda la strana figura del Bonzo e ride*)

IL BONZO

(*a Butterfly, che s'è scostata da tutti*)

Che hai
tu fatto alla Missione?

PINKERTON

Che mi strilla quel matto?

IL BONZO

Rispondi, che hai tu fatto?

And all is settled.
(*The friends surround Butterfly, complimenting her and bowing repeatedly to her.*)

THE GIRLS
Dear Madame Butterfly!

BUTTERFLY
(*raises a finger and corrects*)
No: Madame B. F. Pinkerton.
(*The friends hail Butterfly who kisses some of them; meanwhile the State Official rolls up the scroll and the other papers; then he advises the Imperial Commissary that all is completed.*)

THE COMMISSARY
(*greets Pinkerton*)
Congratulations.

PINKERTON
I thank you for your kindness.

THE COMMISSARY
(*goes up to the Consul*)
Perhaps we'll walk down together?

SHARPLESS
Yes, I'll join you.
(*greets Pinkerton*)
I'll see you tomorrow.
(*shaking hands with Pinkerton*)

PINKERTON
I surely hope so.

REGISTRAR
(*taking leave of Pinkerton*)
May all be sons!

PINKERTON
I'll do my best!
(*The Consul, the Imperial Commissary and the Registrar prepare to return to the city.*)

SHARPLESS
Remember!
(*Pinkerton reassures him with a gesture and waves to him. Sharpless goes down to the path; Pinkerton, in the rear, again waves to him.*)

PINKERTON
(*comes forward again and, rubbing his hands, says to himself*)
Surrounded by my family,
let's not be too discourteous,
and yet: "good riddance." Hip! Hip!

SOPRANO
(*toasting the guests*)
O Kami! O Kami!

PINKERTON
Let's drink to the charming ties that bind us.

YAKUSIDE AND TENORS
O Kami! O Kami!

MOTHER AND AUNT
Let's drink to the lovers!

MOTHER, AUNT, SOPRANOS
O Kami! O Kami!
Let's drink to the charming ties that bind them.
(*The toasts are interrupted by some strange shouting that comes from the path on the hill.*)

BONZO
Cio-Cio-San! Cio-Cio-San!
(*At this cry, all the relatives and friends turn pale and gather together, frightened; Butterfly remains by herself in a corner.*)
What abomination!

BUTTERFLY AND CHORUS
(*horrified*)
Uncle Bonzo!

GORO
(*annoyed by the arrival of Uncle Bonzo*)
Those Bonzos are such bothers!
Is there nobody who could gather him to his fathers?

BONZO
Cio-Cio-San!
(*In the rear the strange figure of Uncle Bonzo appears, preceded by two lantern bearers and followed by two acolytes. Seeing Butterfly who has moved away from all the others, Uncle Bonzo menacingly extends his hands towards her.*)
What did you do at the Mission?

AUNT AND TENORS
Now answer, Cio-Cio-San!

PINKERTON
Why on earth does he yell so?

BONZO
I ask you, will you answer?

TUTTI

Rispondi Cio-cio-san!

IL BONZO

Come, hai tu gli occhi asciutti?
Son dunque questi i frutti?
(urlando)
Ci ha rinnegato tutti!

TUTTI

Hou! Cio-cio-san!

IL BONZO

Rinnegato, vi dico,
il culto antico.

TUTTI

Hou! Cio-cio-san!
(Butterfly si copre il viso vergognosa)

IL BONZO
(gridando sul viso a Butterfly)

Kami sarundasico!
All'anima tua guasta
qual supplizio sovrastra!
(La madre s'interpone per difendere
Butterfly, ma il Bonzo la respinge
brutalmente. Pinkerton infastidito, si
alza e grida al Bonzo:)

PINKERTON

Ehi, dico: basta, basta!
(alla voce di Pinkerton il Bonzo si arresta stupefatto . . . poi con subita
risoluzione invita i parenti e le
amiche a partire)

IL BONZO

Venite tutti. Andiamo!
(a Butterfly)
Ci hai rinnegato e noi . . .

TUTTI

Ti rinneghiamo!

PINKERTON
(autorevolmente)

Sbarazzate all'istante. In casa mia
niente baccano e niente bonzeria.
(Tutti, parenti, amiche, il Bonzo, par-
tono in gran fretta, scendendo la collina e continuando a strillare, imprecare
contro Butterfly. — Le voci a poco a
poco si allontanano. — Butterfly che
è stata sempre immobile e muta colla
faccia nelle mani, scoppia in pianto
infantile. Comincia poco a poco a
calare la sera: poi notte serena e
stellata).

PINKERTON
(va presso Butterfly e con delicatezza le
toglie le mani dal viso)

Bimba, bimba, non piangere
per gracchiar di ranocchi.

BUTTERFLY
(udendo ancora le grida dei parenti, si
tura colle mani le orecchie)

Urlano ancor!

PINKERTON
(rincorandola)

Tutta la tua tribù
e i Bonzi tutti del Giappon non valgono
il pianto di quegli occhi
cari e belli.

BUTTERFLY
(sorridendo infantilmente)

Davver? Non piango più.
E quasi del ripudio non mi duole
per le vostre parole
che mi suonan così dolci nel cuor.

(si china per baciare la mano a Pinkerton)

PINKERTON
(sorpreso a quell' atto, dolcemente lo
impedisce)

Che fai? . . . la man?

BUTTERFLY

Mi han detto
che laggiù fra la gente costumata
è questo il segno del maggior rispetto.

SUZUKI

E Izaghied Izanomi
Sarundasico e Kami.

PINKERTON
(sente un sordo bisbiglio)

Chi brontola lassù?

BUTTERFLY

È Suzuki che fa la sua preghiera
seral.

PINKERTON
(attirandola)

Viene la sera . . .

BUTTERFLY

e l'ombra e la quiete.

PINKERTON

E sei qui sola.

BUTTERFLY

Sola e rinnegata!
Rinnegata e felice!

CHORUS

Yes, answer! Cio-Cio-San!
What's this? You're not even crying?
Is that the way you treat us?
(*shouting*)
She has betrayed her people!
Hou! Cio-Cio-San!

BONZO

She's betrayed, let me tell you, the old
religion.
Kami Sarundasico!
A soul as base and rotten
will be lost and forgotten!
(*cursing Butterfly who has covered her
face with her hands: her mother
comes to defend her but the Bonze
roughly pushes her away and comes
menacingly up to Butterfly, shouting in her face.*)

PINKERTON

(*Losing his patience, he comes between
the Bonze and Butterfly.*)
Enough now! Do you hear me?

BONZO

(*Hearing Pinkerton's voice, the Bonze
stops in surprise, then with a sudden
resolution he asks the relatives and
friends to leave.*)
Yes, we are leaving. Come with me!
(*to Butterfly*)
You have disowned your people.

BONZO AND OTHERS

(*They all go hurriedly to the rear and
raise their arms toward Butterfly.*)
And we disown you!

PINKERTON

(*with authority*)
Go away! Go this moment!
This house is mine,
and I'll have no yelling,
and no one's Bonzo here!
(*At Pinkerton's words they all run hurriedly toward the path that leads to
the city; her mother again tries to go
to Butterfly but is pushed aside by the
others. Uncle Bonzo disappears on
the path that leads to the temple,
followed by the acolytes.*)

PINKERTON

(*Butterfly bursts into tears like a child.
Pinkerton hears her and quickly goes
to her, lifting her up and tenderly re-
moving her hands from her tear-
stained face.*)
Darling, you must not cry, my love!
Never mind how they're croaking.

BUTTERFLY

(*covering her ears to drown out the
cries*)
Hear how they yell!

PINKERTON

(*comforting her*)
All of your loving folks
and all the Bonzos of Japan
are not worth a single tear from
eyes as dear as your eyes.

BUTTERFLY

(*with a child-like smile*)
You're kind.
I'll cry no more.
I even can forget that they've disowned
me:
for your words have consoled me,
I have never heard such sweet words
before. (*bows down to kiss Pinkerton's hand*)

PINKERTON

(*tenderly restraining her*)
Why kiss my hand?

BUTTERFLY

I'm told that where you come from,
among the better people
that's how you show respect and ad-
miration.

SUZUKI

E Izaghied Izanomi Sarundasico, e
Kami.

PINKERTON

(*surprised at the muted whisper*)
Who's murmuring up there?

BUTTERFLY

That's Suzuki:
She says her evening prayers at this
hour.

PINKERTON

Evening is falling,

BUTTERFLY

and darkness and silence.

PINKERTON

You are alone here.

BUTTERFLY

Yes, alone, rejected!
I'm rejected . . . Yet so happy!

PINKERTON

(*ha battuto le mani, ed i servi sono accorsi*)

A voi — chiudete.

BUTTERFLY

(*i servi chiudono le pareti che danno sul terrazo poi si ritirano*)

Sì, sì, noi tutti soli . . .
E fuori il mondo.

PINKERTON
(*ridendo*)

E il Bonzo furibondo.

BUTTERFLY

(*a Suzuki, che è venuta coi servi e sta aspettando gli ordini*)

Suzuki, le mie vesti.

(*Suzuki fruga in un cofano di lacca, mentre Pinkerton guarda i servi che stanno tramutando parte del terrazzo in una camera*)

SUZUKI

(*dopo di aver dato a Butterfly gli abiti per la notte ed un cofanetto coll' occorrente per la toeletta, si inchina innanzi a Pinkerton*)

Buona notte.

(*Aiutata da Suzuki, Butterfly si reca in un angolo al fondo e fa cautelosamente la sua toeletta da notte, levendosi poi la veste nuziale ed indossandone una tutta bianca. Suzuki esce. Pinkerton dondolandosi sulla poltrona e prendendo una sigaretta guarda Butterfly che è intenta ad acconciarsi*)

BUTTERFLY

Quest'obi pomposa
  disciöglier mi tarda
  si vesta la sposa
  di puro candor.
Tra motti sommessi
  sorride . . . mi guarda.
  Celarmi potessi!
  ne ho tanto rossor!
E ancor l'irata
  voce mi maledice . . .
  Butterfly . . . rinnegata
  Rinnegata . . . e felice.

PINKERTON

Con moti di scojattolo
  i nodi allenta e scioglie! . . .
Pensar che quel giocattolo
  è mia moglie. Mia moglie.
Ma tale
  grazia dispiega ch'io
  mi struggo per la febbre
  d'un subito desio.

(*andando verso Butterfly, la solleva e si avvía con essa sul terrazzo esterno*)

Bimba dagli occhi pieni di malìa
ora sei tutta mia.
Sei tutta vestita di giglio.
Mi piace la treccia tua bruna
fra i candidi veli . . .

BUTTERFLY
(*scendendo dal terrazzo*)

Somiglio
la piccola Dea della luna,
la Dea della luna che scende
la notta dal ponte del ciel . . .

PINKERTON (*la segue*)

E affascina i cuori . . .

BUTTERFLY

E li prende,
li avvolge in un bianco mantel.
E via se li reca negli alti reami.

PINKERTON

Ma intanto finor non m'hai detto,
ancor non m'hai detto che m'ami,
Le sa quella Dea le parole
che appagan gli ardenti desir?

BUTTERFLY

Le sa. Forse dirle non vuole
per tema d'averne a morir!

PINKERTON

Stolta paura, l'amor non uccide
ma dà vita, e sorride
per gioie celestiali
come ora fa nei tuoi lunghi occhi ovali.

(*avvicinandosi a lei e prendendole la faccia*)

PINKERTON

(*claps his hands three times; the servants and Suzuki come running, and Pinkerton orders the servants.*)

Suzuki . . . the *shosi*.

(*The servants noiselessly slide some walls.*)

BUTTERFLY

Good, now we are alone here,
the world behind us.

PINKERTON

(*laughing*)

The Bonzo cannot find us!

BUTTERFLY

(*to Suzuki who has come with the servants and stands awaiting her orders*)

Suzuki, bring my robe, please.

(*Suzuki searches in a chest and hands Butterfly her night robe and a little toiletry box.*)

SUZUKI

(*bowing to Pinkerton*)

Good night.

(*Pinkerton claps his hands; the servants hasten away.*)

BUTTERFLY

(*enters the house and, assisted by Suzuki, very carefully completes her night toilette; taking off her wedding robe she garbs herself in a pure white one; then she sits on a cushion and, looking in a mirror, arranges her hair. Suzuki leaves.*)

This elegant *obi* now no longer serves me . . .
the robe of a bride must be white as the moon.
What can he be saying? He smiles and observes me.
And I feel like hiding!
I am so ashamed!

PINKERTON

(*looking at Butterfly lovingly*)

So eager and so coy,
how she scurries like a squirrel!
To think this little toy will be my wife soon.
My wife!
So much loveliness explains
why I'm stricken with the fever
of such a sudden passion.

BUTTERFLY

And yet
I hear that voice and its malediction . . .
"Butterfly! We disown you."
I'm rejected yet so happy!

PINKERTON

(*Getting up, he slowly draws near Butterfly.*)

Girl with those eyes so full of deep enchantment,
you now are mine to cherish!
You're white and as chaste as a lily.
The beautiful strands of your dark hair
make white even whiter.

BUTTERFLY

(*descending from the terrace*)

I look like the Goddess of moonlight,
the frail little Goddess of moonlight
descending from Heaven
when night has arrived.

PINKERTON

All hearts must surrender . . .

BUTTERFLY

She enslaves them
and enfolds them
in lily-white veils,
and takes them to her kingdom,
the realm of the moonlight.

PINKERTON

Remember till now you never told me,
you still have not told me you love me.
Those words, does your goddess not know them,
those words for which lovers all sigh?

BUTTERFLY

She knows them,
but perhaps she won't say them,
for fear if she did, she might die!

PINKERTON

Such fear is foolish,
for love does not kill you.
Love is living,
and its smile is a blessing
sent from Heaven
just like the smile

(*drawing near Butterfly, and caressing her face*)

that now is dancing in your eyes.

(*Butterfly, with a sudden movement, shrinks from Pinkerton's ardent caress.*)

BUTTERFLY

Adesso voi
siete per me l'occhio del firmamento.
E mi piaceste dal primo momento
che vi ho veduto. Siete
alto, forte. Ridete
con modi sì palesi!
E dite cose che mai non intesi.
Or son contenta. Vogliatemi bene,
un bene piccolino,
un bene da bambino
quale a me si conviene.
Noi siamo gente avvezza
alle piccole cose
umili e silenziose,
ad una tenerezza
sfiorante e pur profonda
come il ciel, come l'onda del mare.

PINKERTON

Dammi ch'io baci le tue mani care.

(*prorompe con grande tenerezza*)

Mia Butterfly! . . . come t'han ben
   nomata
tenue farfalla . . .

BUTTERFLY

(*a queste parole si rattrista e ritira le
mani*)

Dicon che oltre mare
se cade in man dell'uom, ogni farfalla
da uno spillo è trafitta
ed in tavola infitta!

PINKERTON

(*riprendendole dolcemente le mani e
sorridendo*)

Un po' di vero c'è.
E tu lo sai perchè?
Perchè non fugga più.

(*abbracciandola*)

Io t'ho ghermita . . .
Ti serro palpitante.
Sei mia.

BUTTERFLY

(*abbandonandosi*)

Sì, per la vita.

PINKERTON

Vieni, vieni.
Via dall'anima in pena
l'angoscia paurosa.

(*indicando a Butterfly il cielo stellato*)

Guarda: è notte serena!
Guarda: dorme ogni cosa!

BUTTERFLY

(*estatica*)

Ah! Dolce notte! Quante stelle!
Non le vidi mai sì belle!
Trema, brilla, ogni favilla
col baglior d'una pupilla.
Oh! quanti occhi fisi, attenti
d'ogni parte a riguardare!
Pei firmamenti,
via pei lidi, via pel mare . . .
Tutto estatico d'amor
ride il cielo.

PINKERTON

(*con cupido amore*)

Vieni, vieni! . . .

(*Butterfly e Pinkerton entrano nella
camera nuziale.*)

ATTO SECONDO

Interno della casetta di Butterfly

*Suzuki prega, raggomitolata davanti
all' immagine di Budda; suona di
quando in quando la campanella
della preghiera. Butterfly sta ritta ed
immobile presso un paravento.*

SUZUKI

(*pregando*)

E Izaghi ed Izanami
Sarundasico e Kami . . .

(*interrompendosi*)

Oh! la mia testa!

(*suona la campanella per richiamare
l'attenzione dei Numi*)

E tu
Ten-Sjoo-daj!

(*guardando Butterfly*)

Fate che Butterfly
non pianga più, mai più,
mai più, mai più.

BUTTERFLY

Now and forever
you'll mean to me
more than the sun in heaven.
And I admit that I liked you
the moment when first I saw you!
You are tall and manly,
your smile is so charming and so easy.
The things you say no one else ever
    told me.
Now I am happy,
I'm very happy.
I beg you to love me,
to love me like a baby,
a tiny, little baby.
That's the way you should love me!
Do love me just a little.
We Japanese are used
to the things that are child-like:
humble and pure and silent.
All our deepest feelings
are tender yet eternal
like the sky,
like the waves of the ocean.

PINKERTON

Give me your lovely hands
that I may kiss them.

(*He exclaims with great tenderness*):
my Butterfly!
How well your name was chosen.
"Butterfly, my darling!"

BUTTERFLY

(*At these words, Butterfly becomes sad
and withdraws her hands.*)

But beyond the ocean
they chase her with a net,
and when they catch her,
put a pin right through her body,
lock her up in a glass case . . .

PINKERTON

(*again taking Butterfly's hands and
smiling*)

That tale is not a lie,
but let me tell you why . . .
so she can't get away!

(*embracing her*)

I now have caught you.
You tremble as I hold you.
You love me!

BUTTERFLY

(*surrendering herself*)

Yes, and forever.

PINKERTON

Come, be mine now!

(*Butterfly shrinks back, as if ashamed
of her abandon.*)

Gone your doubts and your anguish,
your fearful hesitation.

(*pointing to the starry sky*)

The night smiles on lovers!
All the world now is silent . . .

BUTTERFLY

(*ecstatically*)

Ah! night for dreamers!
Stars without number.
All the world has gone to slumber!
Starry heaven! Night so tender!
Beauty makes my heart surrender!
The fragrant flowers yonder
fill the world with silent wonder.
Oh! a silvery moon is shining,
golden stars light up the ocean.
The night is enchanted,
every thing is breathing beauty . . .
And the stars of love
are blinking in the sky!

PINKERTON

(*passionately*)

Be mine! I love you!

(*They go from the garden into the little
house.*)

ACT II

(*The walls are closed, leaving the room
in semi-darkness. Suzuki prays, huddling in front of the image of Buddha;
she intermittently sounds the prayer
bell. Butterfly is lying on the floor
supporting her head in the palms of
her hands.*)

SUZUKI

(*praying*)

E Izaghied Izanami, Sarundasico e
Kami.

(*interrupting herself*)

Ah, how my head hurts!

(*sounds the bell to attract the attention
of the gods*)

And you,
Ten-sjo-o-daj,

(*looking at Butterfly*)

take care of Butterfly,
    that she need cry no more,
        no more!

BUTTERFLY

Pigri ed obesi
son gli Dei giapponesi.
L'americano Iddio son persuasa
ben più presto risponde a chi l'implori.
Ma temo ch'egli ignori
che noi stiam qui di casa.

(*rimane pensierosa, poi si rivolge a Suzuki che si è alzata in piedi ed ha
aperto la parete verso il giardino*)

Suzuki, è lungi la miseria?

SUZUKI

(*apre un piccolo mobile e vi prende
poche monete mostrandole a Butterfly*)

Questo è
l'ultimo fondo.

BUTTERFLY

Questo! Oh! Troppe spese!

SUZUKI

(*ripone il danaro e chiude il piccolo
mobile, mentre sospirando dice:*)

S'egli non torna e presto,
siamo male in arnese.

BUTTERFLY
(*decisa*)

Ma torna.

SUZUKI
(*crollando il capo*)

Tornerà?

BUTTERFLY
(*indispettita a Suzuki*)

Perchè dispose
che il Console provveda alla pigione,
rispondi, su!
Perchè con tante cure
la casa riforni di serrature,
s'ei non volesse ritornar mai più?

SUZUKI

Non lo so.

BUTTERFLY

(*meravigliata a tanta ignoranza*)
Non lo sai?
            (*con orgoglio*)
Io te lo dico. Per tener ben fuori
le zanzare, i parenti ed i dolori

e dentro, con gelosa
custodia, la sua sposa
che son io: Butterfly.

SUZUKI
(*poco convinta*)

Mai non s'è udito
di straniero marito
che sia tornato al suo nido.

BUTTERFLY
(*furibonda*)

Ah! Taci, o t'uccido.

(*insistendo nel persuadere Suzuki*)

Quell'ultima mattina:
tornerete signor? — gli domandai.
Egli, col cuore grosso,
per celarmi la pena
sorridendo rispose:
— O Butterfly
piccina mogliettina,
tornerò colle rose
alla stagion serena
quando fa la nidiata il pettirosso.

(*calma e convinta*)
Tornerà.

SUZUKI
(*con incredulità*)
Speriam.

BUTTERFLY
(*insistendo*)

Dillo con me:
Tornerà.

SUZUKI
(*per compiacerla ripete*)

Tornerà...

(*poi si mette pianger*)

BUTTERFLY
(*sorpresa*)

Piangi? Perchè?
Ah la fede ti manca!

(*poi continua fiduciosa e sorridente*)
Senti —

Un bel dì, vedremo
levarsi un fil di fumo sull'estremo
confin del mare.
E poi la nave appare
E poi la nave bianca
Entra nel porto, romba il suo saluto.

BUTTERFLY

Here in Japan
all our gods are so lazy!
I'm sure, beyond the ocean,
in my new country,
God is faster in answering humble
    prayers.
But then I often wonder
if He knows that we live here.
(*absorbed in thought*) (*Suzuki rises, and
opens the rear wall toward the garden; she goes to a cabinet and opens a
small box, looking for money.*) Suzuki, how long before we're starving?

SUZUKI

That is all we have left now.

BUTTERFLY

That's all?
All those expenses!
(*Suzuki replaces the money in the cabi-
net and closes it.*)

SUZUKI
(*sighing*)

Unless your husband comes back soon,
there'll be nothing but trouble.

BUTTERFLY
(*determined*)

He will come!

SUZUKI
(*shaking her head*)

Are you sure?

BUTTERFLY
(*irritated, coming up to Suzuki*)

Why should he bother
to have the Consul pay our monthly
    rent here?
Why would he, why?
And why would he have troubled
to see to it that all our locks were
    doubled
if he did not intend to come back here?

SUZUKI

I don't know.

BUTTERFLY
(*surprised at so much ignorance*)

You don't know?
(*with confident pride*)

Then I will tell you:
that he did to keep away my folks
and mosquitoes,
and grief and sorrow . . .
and inside,

safe and jealously guarded,
his beloved,
his beloved wife, his sweetheart, But-
    terfly.

SUZUKI
(*unconvinced*)

But have you ever known
an American husband
who did return to the nest?

BUTTERFLY
(*furious*)

Don't say that
or I'll kill you!
(*still intent on convincing Suzuki*)

That morning when he left me:
"will I see you again?"
that's what I asked.
He, though his heart was heavy,
did not want me to know it,
so he smiled as he answered:
"Sweet Butterfly,
my little wife, my darling,
I'll return with the roses,
in that enchanted season
when the red-breasted robin
starts building nests again."
(*calm and confident*)

He'll come back.

SUZUKI
(*incredulously*)

Let's hope so.

BUTTERFLY
(*insisting*)

Say it with me: he'll be back.

SUZUKI
(*To please her, she repeats*)

He'll be back!
(*bursting into tears*)

BUTTERFLY
(*surprised*)

Crying? But why, but why?
Don't you have any faith left?
(*confident and smiling*)

I have.
Soon we'll see
at daybreak
a tiny thread of smoke rise
where the sky
borders on the ocean.
And then a ship in motion.
Gleaming white, it draws near,

Vedi? È venuto!
Io non gli scendo incontro, Io no.
Mi metto
là sul ciglio del colle e aspetto, e aspetto
gran tempo e non mi pesa
la lunga attesa.
E . . . uscito dalla folla cittadina
un uomo, un picciol punto
s'avvia per la collina.
Chi sarà? chi sarà?
E come sarà giunto
che dirà? che dirà?
Chiamerà Butterfly dalla lontana.

Io senza dar risposta
me ne starò nascosta
un po' per celia, e un po' per non
    morire
al primo incontro, ed egli alquanto in
    pena
chiamerà, chiamerà:

*"Piccina mogliettina
olezzo di verbena"*

i nomi che mi dava al suo venire.

(*a Suzuki*)

Tutto questo avverrà, te lo prometto.
Tienti la tua paura — io con sicura
fede l'aspetto.

(*congeda Suzuki*)

(*Suzuki esce dalla porta di sinistra. Butterfly la segue mestamente collo
sguardo*)

(*Nel giardino campaiono Sharpless e
Goro; Goro guarda entro le camera, scorge Butterfly e dice a Sharpless:*)

GORO

C'è. — Entrate.

(*introduce Sharpless; poi torna subito
fuori, e spia di quando in quando dal
giardino*)

S/HARPLESS

(*affacciandosi, bussa discretamente contro la porta di destra*)

Chiedo scusa . . .

(*vede Butterfly che udendo entrare al-
cuno si è mossa*)

Madama Butterfly . . .

BUTTERFLY
(*senza volgersi, ma correggendo*)

Madama Pinkerton
prego.

(*si volge, riconosce il Console e giubilante batte le mani*)

Oh il mio signor Console!

(*Suzuki entra premurosa e prepara un
tavolino coll'occorrente per fumare, alcuni cuscini ed uno sgabello*)

SHARPLESS
(*sorpreso*)

Mi ravvisate?

BUTTERFLY
(*facendo gli onori di casa*)

Benvenuto in casa
americana.

SHARPLESS

Grazie.

BUTTERFLY

(*invita il Console a sedere presso il
tavolino: Sharpless si lascia cadere
grottescamente su di un cuscino: Butterfly si siede dall'altra parte e sorride
con malizia dietro il ventaglio vedendo l'imbarazzo del Console; poi
con molta grazia gli chiede:*)

Avi, antenati
tutti bene?

SHARPLESS
(*sorride ringraziando*)

Ma spero.

BUTTERFLY

(*fa cenno a Suzuki che prepari la pipa*)

Fumate?

SHARPLESS

Grazie.

(*desideroso di spiegare lo scopo per cui
è venuto, cava una lettera di tasca*)

Ho qui . . .

BUTTERFLY
(*gentilmente interrompendolo*)

Signore — io vedo
il cielo azzurro.

(*dopo aver tirato una boccata dalla
pipa che Suzuki ha preparata l'offre
al Console*)

SHARPLESS (*rifiutando*)

Grazie . . .

(*tenta riprendere il suo discorso*)

Ho . . .

steaming into the harbor,
all the guns saluting.
He's come!
Just as I told you!
But I won't go to meet him.
Not yet!
I wander to the rim of the hill-top
and wait there.
I wait for a long time
but I don't mind it,
I'm used to waiting.
A man emerges
from the crowded city,
a dot on the horizon:
he's setting out for our hilltop.
Who on earth
can it be?
And when at last he gets here,
what on earth will he say?
He will call: "Butterfly."
I hear him faintly.
But I don't think I'll answer,
I'll stay a while in hiding:
at first to tease him,
but then for fear
to die in his embraces!
Then worried by my silence
he will call:
"My little wife, my darling,
my fragrant sweet verbena . . ."
the names he used to give me when
first I met him.

(*to Suzuki*)

That's the way it will be,
you may believe me.
You have no right to doubt it
while I with faith unshaken
await him!

(*Butterfly dismisses Suzuki, who exits
through the door at the left. Butterfly gazes after her sadly.*)

(*Goro and Sharpless appear in the
garden; Goro looks into the room,
discovers Butterfly and says to Sharpless who follows him*):

GORO

Yes. She'll see you.

SHARPLESS

(*taps discreetly against the wall at the
rear*)

Beg your pardon . . .

(*Sharpless discovers Butterfly who, on
hearing someone enter, has moved.*)
Is Madame Butterfly . . .

BUTTERFLY

(*Without turning around, she corrects
him.*)

No, Madame Pinkerton, please.

(*She turns and, recognizing the Consul, claps her hands joyfully.*)

Oh! The American gentleman
from the Consulate.

(*Suzuki enters hastily and prepares a
table with all that is needed for a
smoke.*)

SHARPLESS

(*surprised*)

You do remember?

BUTTERFLY

(*welcoming him*)

You're at home here:
this is an American household.

SHARPLESS

Thank you.

(*Butterfly invites the Consul to sit near
the table. Sharpless sits down awk-
wardly on a cushion; Butterfly sits on
the other side, maliciously smiling
behind her fan at the Consul's em-
barrassment; then she asks him very
graciously*):

BUTTERFLY

How are all your forebears?
Well and happy?

SHARPLESS

(*thanks her, smiling*)

I hope so!

BUTTERFLY

(*signals Suzuki to prepare the pipe*)

You smoke?

SHARPLESS

Thank you.

(*wanting to explain the reason for his
visit, takes a letter from his pocket*)
I've got . . .

BUTTERFLY

(*interrupting him*)

Believe me, I am in seventh heaven.

(*After taking a mouthful from the
pipe that Suzuki has prepared, she
offers it to the Consul.*)

SHARPLESS

(*refusing*)

Thank you.

(*still trying to tell his story*) I . . .

BUTTERFLY

(*depone la pipa sul tavolino e assai premurosa dice:*)

Preferite
forse le sigarette

(*ne offre*)

americane.

SHARPLESS

(*ne prende una*)

Grazie.

(*si alza e tenta di continuare il discorso*)

Ho da mostrarvi . . .

BUTTERFLY

(*porge un fiammifero acceso*)

A voi.

SHARPLESS

(*accende la sigaretta, ma poi la depone subito e presentando la lettera si siede sullo sgabello*)

Mi scrisse
Benjamin Franklin Pinkerton . . .

BUTTERFLY

(*premurosissima*)

Davvero!
È in salute?

SHARPLESS

Perfetta.

BUTTERFLY

(*alzandosi, lietissima*)

Io son la donna
più lieta del Giappone. — Potrei favri
una domanda?

(*Suzuki è in faccende per preparare il thè*)

SHARPLESS

Certo.

BUTTERFLY

(*torna a sedere*)

Quando fanno
il lor nido in America
i pettirossi?

SHARPLESS

(*stupito*)

Come dite?

BUTTERFLY

Sì,
prima o dopo di qui?

SHARPLESS

Ma . . . perchè? . . .

(*Goro sale dal terrazo del giardino ed ascolta, non visto, quanto dice Butterfly*)

BUTTERFLY

Mio marito m' ha promesso
di ritornar nella stagion beata
che il pettirosso rifà la nidiata.
Qui l' ha rifatta per ben tre volte, ma
può darsi che di là
usi nidiar men spesso.

(*Goro scoppia in ridere*)

BUTTERFLY

Chi ride?

(*vede Goro*)

Oh, c'è il nakodo.

(*piano a Sharpless*)

Un uom cattivo.

GORO

(*ossequioso, inchinandosi*)

Godo . . .

BUTTERFLY

(*a Goro*)

Zitto.

(*a Sharpless*)

Egli osò . . . No, prima rispondete
alla domanda mia.

SHARPLESS

(*imbarazzato*)

Mi rincresce ma . . . ignoro . . .
Non ho studiato ornitologia.

BUTTERFLY

(*tenta di capire*)

orni . . .

SHARPLESS

. . . tologia.

BUTTERFLY

Non lo sapete
insomma.

SHARPLESS

No.

(*ritenta di tornare in argomento*)

Dicevamo . . .

BUTTERFLY

(*lo interrompe seguendo la sua idea*)

Ah, sì —Goro,
appena B. F. Pinkerton fu in mare,
mi venne ad assediare
con ciarle e con presenti
per ridarmi ora questo or quel marito.
Or promette tesori
per uno scimunito . . .

GORO

(*per giustificarsi, spiega la cosa a Sharpless*)

Il ricco Yamadori.

BUTTERFLY
(*places the pipe on the little table and says solicitously*):
I suppose you'd rather smoke
an American cigaret—yes?
(*offers him some*)

SHARPLESS
(*takes one*)
Well, thank you.
(*He attempts to continue his tale.*)
I've come to read you ...

BUTTERFLY
(*extends Sharpless a lighted match*)
A light.

SHARPLESS
(*lights the cigarette but puts it down immediately and, showing the letter, sits on the stool*)
I've heard from Benjamin Franklin Pinkerton ...

BUTTERFLY
(*very urgently*)
A letter?
And how is he?

SHARPLESS
He's thriving.

BUTTERFLY
(*getting up very joyfully*)
In all Japan there's no happier girl than I am.
(*Suzuki is busy preparing tea.*)
Would you answer me a question?

SHARPLESS
Surely.

BUTTERFLY
(*sits down again*)
In your country,
when do little robins start
to build their new nests?

SHARPLESS
(*astonished*)
Beg your pardon?

BUTTERFLY
Well ... is it later than here?

SHARPLESS
Why on earth?
(*Goro, who is walking about the garden, comes near the terrace and listens, unseen, to what Butterfly is saying.*)

BUTTERFLY
It's because my husband promised
he would return in that enchanted season
when robin red-breast
starts building his new nest.
Here they have made their nests
several time since;
but it could be
that in your country
they nest less often. (*Goro appears and laughs out loud.*)
Who's laughing?
(*seeing Goro*) Oh, that was Goro.
(*softly to Sharpless*) He is a bad man!

GORO
(*advances, and bowing obsequiously*)
Thank you.

BUTTERFLY
(*to Goro*)
Leave us.
(*to Sharpless*) He has dared ... No,
may I first remind you
that I have asked a question?

SHARPLESS
(*embarrassed*)
I can't answer.
I'm sorry.
I'm afraid ornithology escapes me.

BUTTERFLY
Orni ...

SHARPLESS
Ornithology.

BUTTERFLY
That is to say: you don't know!

SHARPLESS
(*attempting to continue*)
Right! We were saying ...

BUTTERFLY
(*interrupts him, pursuing her idea*)
Ah, yes,
Goro, as soon as B. F. Pinkerton had left us,
appeared here every day and
with honeyed words and presents
he suggested each day another husband.
Gold and pearls would be mine
if I took his silly suitor.

GORO
(*intervening to justify himself, enters the room and turns to Sharpless*)
The wealthy Yamadori.

Ella è povera in canna — i suoi
parenti
l'han tutti rinnegata.
(*il Principe Yamadori attraversa il giardino seguito da due servi che portano fiori*)

BUTTERFLY
(*vede Yamadori e lo indica a Sharpless sorridendo*)
Eccolo. Attenti.
(*Yamadori entra con grande imponenza, fa un graziosissimo inchino a Butterfly poi saluta il Console. I due servi consegnano i fiori a Suzuki e si ritirano nel fondo. Goro, servilissimo, porta uno sgabello a Yamadori, fra Sharpless e Butterfly, ed è dappertutto durante la conversazione. Sharpless e Yamadori siedono*)
(*a Yamadori*)
Yamadori — ancor . . . le pene
dell'amor non v'han deluso?
Vi tagliate ancor le vene
se il mio bacio vi ricuso?

YAMADORI
(*a Sharpless*)
Tra le cose più moleste
è l' inutil sospirar.

BUTTERFLY
(*con graziosa malizia*)
Tante mogli omai toglieste,
vi doveste abituar.

YAMADORI
L' ho sposate tutte quante
e il divorzio mi francò.

BUTTERFLY
Obbligata.

YAMADORI
(*premuroso*)
A voi però
giurerei fede costante

SHARPLESS
(*sospirando, rimette in tasca la lettera*)
(Il mio messaggio
a trasmetter non riesco.)

GORO
(*con enfasi indicando Yamadori a Sharpless*)
Ville, servi, oro, ad Omura
un palazzo principesco.

BUTTERFLY
(*con serietà*)
Già legata è la mia fede.

GORO E YAMADORI
(*a Sharpless*)
Maritata ancor si crede.

BUTTERFLY
(*con forza*)
Non mi credo — sono — sono.

GORO
Ma la legge . . .

BUTTERFLY
(*interrompendolo*)
Io non la so.

GORO
(*continua*)
. . . per la moglie, l'abbandono
al divorzio equiparò.

BUTTERFLY
(*crollando vivamente il capo*)
La legge giapponese . . .
non gia del mio paese.

GORO
Quale?

BUTTERFLY
(*con forza*)
Gli Stati Uniti.

SHARPLESS
(Oh, l' infelice!)

BUTTERFLY
(*nervosissima, accalorandosi*)
Si sa che aprir la porta
e la moglie cacciar per la più corta
qui divorziar si dice.
Ma in America questo non si può.
(*a Sharpless*)
Vero?

SHARPLESS
(*imbarazzato*)
Vero . . . Però . . .

BUTTERFLY
(*lo interrompe rivolgendosi a Yamadori ed a Goro, trionfante*)
Là un bravo giudice
serio, impettito
dice al marito:
"Lei vuol andarsene?
Sentiam perchè?"
"Sono seccato
del coniugato!"
E il magistrato:
"Ah, mascalzone,
presto in prigione!"
(*e per troncare si alza ed ordina:*)
Suzuki, il thè.
(*va anche lei presso Suzuki*)

The poor girl is in trouble,
for all her relatives disown her
and despise her. (*Outside on the terrace, Prince Yamadori arrives in a
sedan chair, attended by servants.*)

BUTTERFLY
(*sees Yamadori and points him out to
Sharpless, smiling*)
There he is . . .
please, watch him.
(*Yamadori, welcomed by Goro bowing,
gets down from the sedan chair,
greets the Consul and Butterfly, who
has advanced to the rear wall; Yamadori sits on the terrace, turns respectfully towards Butterfly who
kneels in the room.*)
(*to Yamadori*)
Yamadori, you still are sighing: you
adore me,
and how you miss me!
Any day they'll find you dying
if I shall not let you kiss me.

YAMADORI
Nothing keeps me quite so harried
as to sigh and woo in vain.

BUTTERFLY
(*slyly, though graciously*)
After all the wives you've married,
why attempt it once again?

YAMADORI
Every single time I married
I was granted a divorce.

BUTTERFLY
I'm encouraged!

YAMADORI
I can assure you with you it would be
different.

SHARPLESS
(*sighing, he returns the letter to his
pocket*)
(If he carries on much longer,
she will never hear the letter.)

GORO
(*emphatically pointing to Yamadori*)
Houses, servants, treasures,
in Omara you'd have a princely palace.

BUTTERFLY
(*seriously*)
But you know I'm bound forever.

GORO AND YAMADORI
(*to Sharpless*)
She still thinks that she is married.

BUTTERFLY
I don't think so: no!
I know it.

GORO
But the law says . . .

BUTTERFLY
There's no such law.

GORO
once a wife has been abandoned,
that amounts to a divorce.

BUTTERFLY
That may be Japanese law
but not the law of my country.

GORO
Which one?

BUTTERFLY
The U.S.A. law.

SHARPLESS
(Poor little woman!)

BUTTERFLY
(*very nervous, growing excited*)
Here, husbands are not queasy.
"Had enough! Send her packing,
it's so easy!"
That's what they call divorce here.
But in America
things are very different.
(*to Sharpless*)
Right, Sir?

SHARPLESS
(*embarrassed*)
Surely. And yet . . .

BUTTERFLY
(*interrupts him, turning to Yamadori
and Goro, triumphantly*)
There they have judges
to deal with such scoundrels.
One of them asks him:
"You want to leave your wife? May I
ask why?"
"Married life bores me,
so please divorce me!"
What does the judge say?
"Ah, that's what you think!
Two years in prison!"
(*to change the subject, she orders
Suzuki*) Let's have some tea. (*Butterfly goes toward Suzuki, who has
already prepared the tea and is pour-
ing it into the cups.*)

YAMADORI

(sottovoce a Sharpless, mentre Butterfly prepara il thè)

Udiste?

SHARPLESS

Mi rattrista una si piena
cecità.

GORO

(sottovoce a Sharpless e Yamadori)

Segnalata è già la nave
di Pinkerton.

YAMADORI

(disperato)

Quand'essa lo riveda . . .

SHARPLESS

(pure sottovoce ai due)

Egli non vuol mostrarsi. — Io venni
   appunto
per levarla d'inganno.

(vedendo Butterfly che si avvicina per
offrire il thè, tronca il discorso)

BUTTERFLY

(con grazia, servendo a Sharpless una
tazza di thè)

Vostra Grazia permette . . .

(poi apre il ventaglio e dietro a questo
accenna ai due, ridendo)

Che persone moleste!

(offre il thè a Yamadori, che rifiuta)

YAMADORI

(sospirando si alza e si inchina a Butterfly, mettendo la mano sul cuore)

Addio. Vi lascio il cuor pien di cor-
   doglio:
ma spero ancor.

BUTTERFLY

Padrone.

YAMADORI

(s'avvia, poi torna presso Butterfly)

Ah! se voleste . . .

BUTTERFLY

Il guaio è che non voglio . . .

(Yamadori sospira di nuovo: saluta
Sharpless, poi se ne va, seguito dai
servi. Butterfly fa cenno a Suzuki di
preparare il thè: Suzuki eseguisce,
poi va in fondo alla camera. Goro
segue premurosamente Yamadori)

SHARPLESS

(assume un fare grave, serio, però con
gran rispetto e con una certa com-
mozione invita Butterfly a sedere, e
torna a tirar fuori di tasca la lettera)

Ora a noi. — Sedete qui,

(Butterfly, tutta allegra, siede vicino a
Sharpless, che gli presenta la lettera)

legger con me volete
questa lettera?

BUTTERFLY

Date.

(prende la lettera, la bacia e poi se la
mette sul cuore)

Sulla bocca, sul cuore . . .

(rende la lettera a Sharpless e gli dice
graziosamente:)

Siete l'uomo migliore
del mondo. — Incominciate.

SHARPLESS

(legge)

"Amico cercherete
quel bel fior di fanciulla . . ."

BUTTERFLY

(interrompendolo con gioia)

Dice proprio così?

SHARPLESS

Sì, così dice,
ma se ad ogni momento . . .

BUTTERFLY

(rimettendosi tranquilla)

Taccio, taccio — più nulla.

SHARPLESS

(riprende)

"Da quel tempo felice
tre anni son passati."

BUTTERFLY

(non può trattenersi)

Anche lui li ha contati.

SHARPLESS

(continua)

"E forse Butterfly
non mi rammenta più."

BUTTERFLY

(sorpresa)

Non lo rammento?

(rivolgendosi a Suzuki)

Suzuki, dillo tu.

(ripete come scandolezzata le parole
della lettera)

"Non mi rammenta più!"

(Suzuki accenna affermando, poi entra
nella stanza a sinistra)

YAMADORI
(*whispering to Sharpless*)
You heard her?

SHARPLESS
(*whispering*)
It is saddening
to see how blind a girl can be.

GORO
(*whispering to Sharpless and Yamadori*)
By the way, they tell me
Pinkerton's ship is due.

YAMADORI
(*desperate*)
The moment that she sees him . . .

SHARPLESS
(*whispering to the two*)
He does not want to see her.
It was the purpose of my visit
to prepare her.
(*Seeing that Butterfly, followed by Suzuki, is approaching with the tea, he
breaks off the conversation.*)

BUTTERFLY
(*offering tea to Sharpless*)
Will you please have some tea now?
(*opens the fan and behind it, points to
the two, laughing*)
Ah! those two are a nuisance!

YAMADORI
(*gets up to leave*)
Farewell, then.
(*sighing*)
Please keep my heart;
though it is broken,
I won't despair.

BUTTERFLY
Your Lordship.

YAMADORI
(*about to depart, he returns, going
toward Butterfly.*)
Ah, if you wanted . . .

BUTTERFLY
The trouble is I don't!
(*Yamadori, after having greeted Sharpless, sighs, leaves, enters the sedan
chair and departs, followed by his
servants and Goro. Butterfly continues
to laugh behind her fan. Sharpless sits
on the stool with an intentionally
grave bearing; respectfully and rather
emotionally he invites Butterfly to be
seated, and again takes the letter
from his pocket.*)

SHARPLESS
Now to us:
sit down right here.
(*showing the letter*)
You and I will read
this letter here from Pinkerton.

BUTTERFLY
(*taking the letter*)
Please, Sir:
(*kissing it*)
let me kiss it,
(*putting it to her heart*)
and hug it . . .
(*to Sharpless, tenderly*)
You're the kindliest man in the whole
world!
(*hands him the letter and sits very attentively*)
But now let's read it.

SHARPLESS
(*reading*)
"Dear Sharpless, have a few words
with that sweetest of flowers."

BUTTERFLY
(*cannot contain herself and exclaims
joyfully*)
Are those really his words?

SHARPLESS
Yes, those are his words;
but if you interrupt me . . .

BUTTERFLY
(*Becoming quiet again, she continues
listening.*)
I'll be silent, I promise.

SHARPLESS
"Since that happiest of springtimes
three years have passed already . . .

BUTTERFLY
(*interrupts his reading*)
He has counted them also!

SHARPLESS
(*continuing*)
and maybe Butterfly
remembers me no more."

BUTTERFLY
(*surprised, turning to Suzuki*)
Do I remember?
Suzuki, did you hear?
(*repeats, quite outraged, the words of
the letter*)
"Remembers me no more."
(*Suzuki exits through the door at the
left, carrying away the tea.*)

SHARPLESS
(*fra sè*)

(Pazienza!)

(*seguita a leggere*)

"Se mi vuole
bene ancora, se m' aspetta . . ."

BUTTERFLY
(*assai commossa*)

Oh le dolci parole!

(*prende la lettera e la bacia*)

Tu, benedetta!

SHARPLESS

(*riprende la lettera e seguita a leggere
imperterrito, ma con voce commossa*)

"A voi mi raccomando
perchè vogliate con circospezione
prepararla . . ."

BUTTERFLY
(*ansiosa e raggiante*)

Ritorna . . .

SHARPLESS

"al colpo . . ."

BUTTERFLY
(*salta di gioia e batte le mani*)

Quando?
Presto! presto!

SHARPLESS

(*rassegnato piega la lettera e la ripone
in tasca*)

(Benone.
Qui troncarla conviene . . .

(*crollando il capo arrabbiato*)

Quel diavolo d'un Pinkerton!)

(*si alza e seriissimo guardando negli occhi Butterfly, le dice:*)

Ebbene,
che fareste Madama Butterfly
s'ei non dovesse ritornar più mai?

BUTTERFLY

(*immobile, come colpita a morte, china
la testa e dice con sommessione infantile:*)

Due cose potrei fare:
tornare a divertire
la gente col cantare
oppur, meglio, morire.

SHARPLESS

(*vivamente commosso passeggia agitatissimo, poi torna verso Butterfly, le
prende le due mani e con paterna
tenerezza le dice:*)

Di strapparvi assai mi costa
dai miraggi ingannatori.
Accogliete la proposta
di quel ricco Yamadori.

BUTTERFLY
(*ritirando le mani*)

Voi, signor, mi dite questo! Voi?

SHARPLESS
(*imbarazzato*)

Santo Iddio, come si fa?

BUTTERFLY
(*batte le mani; Suzuki accorre*)

Qui, Suzuki, presto presto,
che Sua Grazia se ne va.

SHARPLESS

Mi scacciate?

(*fa per avviarsi, ma Butterfly corre a
lui singhiozzando e lo trattiene*)

BUTTERFLY

Ve ne prego,
già l'insistere non vale.

(*congeda Suzuki, la quale va nel giardino*)

SHARPLESS
(*scusandosi*)

Fui brutale, non lo nego.

BUTTERFLY

(*dolorosamente, portandosi la mano al
cuore*)

Oh, mi fate tanto male,
tanto male, tanto, tanto!

(*Butterfly vacilla; Sharpless fa per sorreggerla*)

(*subito dominandosi*)

Niente, niente!
Ho creduto morir. — Ma passa presto
come passan le nuvole sul mare . . .

SHARPLESS
(to himself)

(I thought so!)

(continues reading)

"If she's still fond of me,
and expects me . . ."

BUTTERFLY
(with great tenderness)

Only he knows such sweet words!

(kissing the letter)

My darling, bless you.

SHARPLESS

(takes back the letter and continues to
read it unperturbed, but his voice
trembles with emotion)

"I trust you will oblige me,
and when you see her,
have a little talk with her and try to . . .

BUTTERFLY
(excited, but happy)

He's coming!

SHARPLESS
. . . prepare her . . ."

BUTTERFLY

(She rises, overcome with joy, and claps
her hands.)

Tell me! Quickly! Tell me!

SHARPLESS

(That does it!

(gets up suddenly and returns the letter
to his pocket)

I must tell her the truth now.
The devil take that Pinkerton!)

(looks Butterfly in the eyes, very seriously)

I ask you what you would do,
Madame Butterfly,
if you should find
that he will not return?

(Butterfly remains motionless as though
mortally wounded, bends her head
and replies with childlike submissive-
ness, almost stammering.)

BUTTERFLY

Two things I could do:
I could . . .
I could go back and sing and dance
again . . .
or else . . . better . . . I'd die.

SHARPLESS

(Sharpless is genuinely touched and
walks agitatedly up and down, then
he returns to Butterfly, takes her two
hands, and with paternal tenderness,
says to her):

How I hate to be so cruel
to destroy a fond illusion,
but I think you ought to listen
to that wealthy Yamadori.

BUTTERFLY
(withdrawing her hands)

You, you, a friend,
you dare to say this? You?

SHARPLESS
(embarrassed)

Lord in Heaven, what can I do?

BUTTERFLY

(claps her hands and Suzuki comes
running)

Come, Suzuki, hurry, hurry—
our guest would like to leave.

SHARPLESS
(prepares to depart)

You dismiss me?

BUTTERFLY

(Butterfly, repentant, runs to Sharpless
and sobbingly detains him.)

I don't mean to,
but it's useless to continue.

(dismisses Suzuki who goes into the garden)

SHARPLESS
(excusing himself)

I was brutal—I regret it.

BUTTERFLY

(sorrowfully placing her hand on her
heart)

You don't know
how much you hurt me,
ah, you hurt me, deeply, deeply!

(Butterfly falters, Sharpless moves to
assist her but Butterfly immediately
regains her composure.)

Nothing, nothing!
I was sure I would die. . .
It's passed already,
passed as swiftly as clouds above the
ocean.

Ah! . . . mi ha scordata?

*(corre nella stanza di sinistra, rientra
trionfalmente tenendo il suo bambino
seduto sulla spalla e lo mostra a
Sharpless gloriandosene)*

E questo? . . . e questo? . . . e questo
egli potrà pure scordare? . . .

*(depone il bambino a terra e lo tiene
stretto a sè)*

SHARPLESS
(con emozione)

Egli è suo?

BUTTERFLY
(indicando mano, mano)

Chi vide mai
a bimbo del Giappone occhi azzurrini?
E il labbro? E i ricciolini
d'oro schietto?

SHARPLESS
(sempre più commosso)

È palese.
E . . . Pinkerton lo sa?

BUTTERFLY

No. È nato quand' egli stava
in quel suo gran paese.

(accarezza il suo bambino)

Ma voi gli scriverete che l' aspetta
un figlio senza pari!
e mi saprete dir s' ei non s' affretta
per le terre e pei mari!

*(fa sedere il bimbo sul cuscino e lo ba-
cia teneramente)*

Sai tu cos' ebbe cuore

(gli indica Sharpless)

di pensar quel signore?
Che tua madre dovrà
prenderti in braccio ed alla pioggia e
    al vento
andar per la città
a guadagnarti il pane e il vestimento.
E alle impietosite
genti, la man tremante stenderà!
Gridando: "Udite, udite
la triste mia canzon.

A un infelice madre la carità,
muovetevi a pietà."
E Butterfly, orribile destino,
danzerà per te!
E come fece già — la Geisha canterà!

(mostrando il bimbo e carezzandolo)

E la canzon giuliva e lieta
in un singhiozzo finirà!
Ah! No! No! questo mai!
Questo mestier che al disonore porta!
Morta! Morta! Mai più danzar!
Piuttosto la mia vita vo' troncar!
Ah! morta!

*(mette la sua guancia presso la guancia
del bimbo)*

SHARPLESS
(non può trattenere lagrime)

(Quanta pietà!)

*(poi, vincendo la propria emozione,
dice:)*

Io scendo al piano.
*(Butterfly si alza in piedi e con atto
gentile dà la mano a Sharpless, che la
stringe con ambe le mani con effu-
sione)*

Mi perdonate?

BUTTERFLY
(al bimbo)

A te, dagli la mano.

SHARPLESS
(prende il bambino in braccio)

I bei capelli biondi!

(lo bacia)

Caro: come ti chiamano?

BUTTERFLY

Rispondi:
oggi il mio nome è: *Dolore.* Però
dite al babbo, scrivendogli, che il giorno
del suo ritorno
Gioia mi chiamerò.

SHARPLESS

Tuo padre lo saprà, te lo prometto.

*(mette il bambino in terra, fa un saluto
a Butterfly, ed esce rapidamento)*

(very resolutely)
Ah! he forgot me?
*(Butterfly leaves and re-enters trium-
phantly, carrying her child on her
left shoulder, showing him to Sharpless proudly.)*
And this one? And this one?
This child here,
maybe it, too, will be forgotten?
*(puts the child on the floor and holds
him close to her)*

SHARPLESS
(with emotion)
Is it his?

BUTTERFLY
(pointing, as she asks)
In all Japan, have you ever seen
a baby with such blue eyes,
such lips,
with curls so golden and so silken?

SHARPLESS
(increasingly moved)
Yes, it's obvious.
Is Pinkerton aware?

BUTTERFLY
No. No. When he came
my darling husband was far away already.
(caressing the child)
But surely now you will write him
that the handsomest boy on earth
awaits him!
As soon as he hears that,
he will come flying
over mountains, over oceans!
*(Seating the child on her cushion and
kneeling near him, she kisses the baby
tenderly.)*
You will never guess, my love,
what he has asked your mother:
(pointing to Sharpless)
He has asked her
to fold your arms around her
and through the downpour,
through wind and storm
to roam the town,
earning enough
to buy you bread and clothing,
and to a crowd of heartless people
stretch out a trembling begging hand
and cry out:
"I beg you, good people,
do listen to my song,
and to a hapless mother

do not deny the charity she craves!"
And Butterfly,
condemned by cruel fate,
will start to dance again,
as in the olden times,
(taking the child in her arms)
the Geisha sings once more.
And then her gay little light-hearted
song
will end in sobs and anguished tears.
*(falls to the floor near the child whom
she embraces and caresses, with con-
vulsive emotion)*
Ah!
No! No! Not again!
That hateful trade shall not again dis-
grace me!
Kill me! Kill me!
I will not dance!
If that's my only choice,
I'd rather die!
(hugging the baby)
Ah! Die!
*(She presses the child to her heart and
then falling to the ground next to
him embraces him passionately.)*

SHARPLESS
(cannot hold back his tears)
(She breaks my heart).
(holding his emotions in check)
I say goodbye now.
Can you forgive me?
*(Butterfly gently gives her hand to
Sharpless, who holds it in his with
affection.)*

BUTTERFLY
(turning to the child)
My boy, give him your hand.

SHARPLESS
How blond his pretty curls are!
Tell me: what is your name, my love?

BUTTERFLY
You answer:
Now my name still is Sorrow.
But, please, write my father
and say to him:
the moment that he returns here
Happy, Happy
shall be my name!

SHARPLESS
Yes, I shall tell him that,
it is a promise.
*(He greets Butterfly and exits rapidly
from the door at the right.)*

BUTTERFLY
(battendo le mani)

Suzuki.

SUZUKI
(di fuori grida)

Vespa! Rospo maledetto!

*(poi entra trascinando con violenza
Goro, che tenta inutilmente di sfug-
girle)*

BUTTERFLY

Che fu?

SUZUKI

Ci ronza intorno
il vampiro! e ogni giorno
ai quattro venti
spargendo va
che niuno sa
chi padre al bimbo sia!

*(Suzuki lascia Goro, il quale tenta di
giustificarsi)*

GORO

Dicevo . . . solo . . . che là
in America
quando un figliolo è nato maledetto
trarrà sempre reietto la vita
fra le genti!

*(Butterfly, furente, corre al reliquiario
e prende il coltello che servì per
l'hari-kari—suicidio per condanna—
di suo padre, gridando:)*

BUTTERFLY

Ah! tu menti! menti!

*(afferra Goro, che cade a terra, e mi-
naccia d' ucciderlo: Goro grida dis-
peratamente)*

Dillo ancora e t'uccido! . . .

SUZUKI
(intromettendosi)

No!

*(spaventata a tale scena prende il bim-
bo e lo porta nella stanza a sinistra)*

BUTTERFLY
*(presa da disgusto, respinge Goro col
piede)*

Va via!

*(Goro fugge: poi Butterfly si scuote, va
a riporre il coltello e volgendo il pensiero al suo bambino, esclama:)*

Vedrai, piccolo amore,
mia pena e mio conforto,
il tuo vendicatore
ci porterà lontan nella sua terra.

(un colpo di cannone)

SUZUKI
(entrando affannosamente)

Il cannone del porto!

*(corre verso il terrazzo: Butterfly la
segue)*

Una nave da guerra . . .

BUTTERFLY
(giubilante, ansante)

Bianca . . . bianca . . . il vessillo americano
delle stelle . . . Or governa
per ancorare.

*(prende sul tavolino un cannocchiale e
corre sul terrazzo: tutta tremante per
l' emozione, appunta il cannocchiale
verso il porto e dice a Suzuki:)*

Reggimi la mano
ch'io ne discerna
il nome, il nome, il nome. Eccolo:
ABRAMO LINCOLN!

*(dà il cannocchiale a Suzuki, poi in
preda a grande esaltazione scendendo
dal terrazzo esclama:)*

Tutti han mentito!
tutti! . . . tutti! . . . sol io
lo sapevo — io — che l' amo.

(a Suzuki)

Vedi lo scimunito
tuo dubbio? È giunto! è giunto!
proprio nel punto
che ognun diceva: piangi e dispera.
Trionfa il mio
amor, la mia fè trionfa intera.
Ei torna e m'ama!

*(e in preda ad una esaltazione giubi-
lante va al terrazzo, dicendo a
Suzuki:)*

Scuoti quella fronda di ciliegio
e m'innonda di fior.
Io vo' tuffare nella pioggia odorosa
l'arsa fronte.

(singhiozzando per tenerezza)

SUZUKI
(calmandola)

Signora, quetatevi: quel pianto . . .

BUTTERFLY

No: rido, rido! Quanto
lo dovremo aspettare?
Che pensi? Un' ora?

SUZUKI
(outside, crying out)
Viper! Serpent! Cursed liar!
(Suzuki enters, violently dragging Goro,
who vainly attempts to flee from her.
Goro cries out.)

BUTTERFLY
(to Suzuki)
What now?

SUZUKI
He is a reptile
spewing poison!
From dawn to midnight
he whispers slander
and tells the world
that no one knows
who's child your little boy is!
(leaving Goro)

GORO
I tell them only the truth:
in America a child like this one,
a child born out of wedlock
will always be an outcast
among the decent people!

BUTTERFLY
(runs to the reliquary and seizes the
knife hanging there)
Ah! You liar! Liar! Liar! Ah! liar!
(She seizes Goro, who falls to the floor,
and threatens to kill him. Goro emits
loud prolonged cries of fear.)
One more word and I'll kill you!

SUZUKI
(intervening; then, frightened at the
scene, takes the child to the room at
the left)
No!

BUTTERFLY
(overcome with disgust)
Get out!
(Goro flees. Butterfly remains motionless as if turned to stone. Little by
little she stirs again and replaces
the knife. Overcome, she turns her
thoughts to her child.)
You'll see, my little boy,
my sorrow and consolation,
my darling, my life.
Ah! very soon now
your father will return.
I know he'll come,
he'll come back and take us to his
    country,
he'll take us far away!
(a cannon shot)

SUZUKI
(enters excited)
That's the gun in the harbor!
(Butterfly and Suzuki run toward the
terrace.)
I believe it's a warship.

BUTTERFLY
Big . . . white . . .
with a U.S. flag;
I see the Stars and Stripes.
I believe they are casting anchor!
(takes a telescope from the little table
and runs to the terrace to look)
Hold my trembling hand
so that I may read the name . . . the
    name.
(trembling with emotion, she points the
telescope towards the harbor and says
to Suzuki):
Do help me!
Here it is: Abraham Lincoln!
(gives the telescope to Suzuki and re-
enters the room in a state of great
exaltation)
All have been lying, lying, lying . . .
and I only knew the truth
because I love him.
(to Suzuki)
Now do you see
how silly your doubts were?
He did come! My husband!
He came back just at the moment
when all were saying:
there is no hope left!
I never despaired for I knew
that my faith would be triumphant
because he loves me!
(Jubilantly, she runs to the terrace.)
(to Suzuki who has followed her onto
the terrace)
Ask the cherry-tree
to yield its blossoms,
drown my face in its flowers,
and let me cool
in that sweetest of rains
my burning forehead.
(sobbing with tenderness)

SUZUKI
(calming her)
Compose yourself,
I beg of you . . . your weeping . . .

BUTTERFLY
No: laughing, laughing!
How much longer must we still wait,
    Suzuki?
One hour?

SUZUKI

Di più.

BUTTERFLY
(*giudiziosa*)

Due ore forse. Tutto sia pien
di fior, come la notte è di faville.
Va pei fior.

(*accenna a Suzuki di andare nel
giardino*)

SUZUKI
(*dal terrazzo*)

Tutti i fior? . . .

BUTTERFLY

Tutti. Pesco, viola, gelsomino,
quanto di cespo, o d' erba, o d' albero
fiorì.

SUZUKI

Uno squallor d' inverno sarà tutto il
giardino.

(*scende nel giardino*)

BUTTERFLY

Tutta la primavera voglio che olezzi
qui.

SUZUKI

(*appare sul terrazzo e sporge un fascio
di fiori e di fronde*)

A voi signora.

BUTTERFLY
(*prendendo il fascio*)

Cogline ancora.

(*Butterfly sparge i fiori nella stanza,
mentre Suzuki ritorna nel giardino*)

SUZUKI
(*dal giardino*)

Soventi a questa siepe veniste a
riguardare
lungi, piangendo nella deserta immen-
sità.

BUTTERFLY

Giunse l'atteso, nulla più chiedo al
mare;
diedi pianto alla zolla, essa i suoi fior
mi dà.

SUZUKI

(*appare nuovamente sul terrazzo con
un altro gran fascio di fiori*)

Spoglio è l'orto

BUTTERFLY
(*prendendo i fiori*)

Spoglio è l'orto.
Vien, m' aiuta.

(*spargono fiori ovunque*)

SUZUKI

Rose al varco
della soglia.

BUTTERFLY

Il suo sedil
di convolvi s' inghirlandi.

SUZUKI

Gigli? . . . viole? . . .

BUTTERFLY

intorno spandi.

BUTTERFLY E SUZUKI

Seminiamo intorno april.

(*con leggero ondulamento di danza
spargono ovunque fiori*)

Gettiamo a mani piene
mammole e tuberose,
corolle di verbene
petali d' ogni fior!

(*Butterfly, aiutata da Suzuki va a prendere il necessario per la toeletta*)

SUZUKI

So soon?

BUTTERFLY

Two hours, maybe.
Flowers, flowers,
a sea of bloom,
as many flowers as stars in heaven.
(*signals Suzuki to go into the garden*)
Bring them here.

SUZUKI

(*from the terrace*)

All the flowers?

BUTTERFLY

All the flowers!
Jasmin, peach and cherry blossoms.
Every sweetest radiant flower,
every fragrant bloom.

SUZUKI

(*in the garden at the foot of the
terrace*)

As in the depth of winter's cold
your trees will all be bare!

BUTTERFLY

Give me the scent of spring-time,
let me have my spring in this room.

SUZUKI

As in the depth of winter
your trees will all be bare.
Here are your flowers.
(*appears at the foot of the terrace with
a bouquet of flowers, which she
hands to Butterfly*)

BUTTERFLY

(*taking the flowers from Suzuki's
hands*)

That's not enough yet.
(*Butterfly puts the flowers into the
vases, while Suzuki returns to the
garden.*)

SUZUKI

(*from the garden*)

How often in this garden
you stood forlorn and waiting,
longing and crying,
staring into immensity.

BUTTERFLY

Now he is returning
over that self-same ocean.
I gave my tears to the earth,
now earth returns flowers to me.

SUZUKI

(*again appears on the terrace, her arms
full of flowers*)

No more flowers.

BUTTERFLY

No more flowers?
Come and help me.

SUZUKI

Let's put roses on the threshold.
(*Butterfly and Suzuki scatter flowers
everywhere.*)

BUTTERFLY

Give me the scent of springtime,
let us have spring in here!

SUZUKI

Here is the scent of springtime;
let us have spring in here.

BUTTERFLY

Fill the house with April showers,
with the scent of spring.
Give me the scent of April,
let me have my spring in here!

SUZUKI

Here is the scent of April
with its flowers.
Lilies? Jasmin?

BUTTERFLY

We will be drowned in fragrant
showers.

SUZUKI

Fill the room with April bloom.

BUTTERFLY

Fill the house with April bloom.
Let us be drowned in April showers,
jasmin and violets,
thousands of flowers,
lilies and roses, cherry blossoms;
let us spread the scent of spring!

SUZUKI

Lilies and fragrant roses,
all of the bloom of springtime,
jasmin, lovely roses;
let us spread the scent of spring!

BUTTERFLY AND SUZUKI

(*They throw flowers, and their bod-
ies follow the rhythm of their move-
ments in a quiet dance.*)

A balm from hands caressing,
violets, tuberoses,
the springtime's tender blessing,
petals of every flower.
(*Suzuki places two lamps near the
dressing table where Butterfly is huddling.*)

BUTTERFLY
(a Suzuki)

Or vienmi ad adornar . . .
No! Pria portami il bimbo.
(Suzuki va nella stanza a sinistra e porta il bambino che fa sedere vicino a
Butterfly, la quale, intanto, si guarda
in un piccolo specchio e dice triste-
mente:)
Non son più quella!
Troppi sospiri la bocca mandò,
e l'occhio riguardò
nel lontan troppo fisso.
(si alza, torna alla toeletta e dice a
Suzuki:)
Dammi sul viso
un tocco di carmino . . .
(prende un pennello e mette del rosso
sulle guancie del suo bimbo)
ed anche a te, piccino,
perchè la veglia non ti faccia vôte
per pallore le gote.

SUZUKI
(a Butterfly)

Non vi movete che v'ho a
ravviare i capelli.

BUTTERFLY
(segundo una sua idea)

Che ne diranno! . . .
E lo zio Bonzo?
Già del mio danno
tutti contenti!
E Yamadori
coi suoi languori!
    Beffati,
    scornati,
    spennati
    gl' ingrati!

SUZUKI
(ha terminato la toeletta)

È fatto.

BUTTERFLY

L' obi che vestii da sposa.
(Suzuki va ad un cassettone e vi cerca
la veste, mentre Butterfly attira a sè
il bambino)

BUTTERFLY
(depone il bimbo)

Qua ch'io lo vesta.
(mentre indossa la veste, Suzuki mette
l' altra al bambino, avvolgendolo quasi
tutto nella pieghe ampie e leggiere)
Vo' che mi veda indosso
il vel del primo dì.
E un papavero rosso
nei capelli . . .

(Suzuki, che ha finito d'abbigliare il
bambino, cerca il fiore e lo punta nei
capelli di Butterfly, che se ne compia-
ce, guardandosi nello specchio)

Così.

(poi fa cenno a Suzuki di chiudere lo
shosi)

Nello shosi farem tre forellini
per riguardar,
e starem zitti come topolini
ad aspettar.

(Porta il bambino presso lo shosi, nel
quale fa tre fori: uno alto per sè, uno
più basso per Suzuki e il terzo ancor
più basso pel bimbo, che fa sedere su
di un cuscino, accennandogli di guardare attento fuori del foro prepara-
togli. Suzuki si accoscia e spia essa
pure all'esterno. Butterfly si pone innanzi al foro più alto e spia da quello. Dopo qualche tempo Suzuki ed il
bambino si addormentano. Intanto si
è fatta notte ed i raggi lunari illu-
minano dall'esterno lo shosi. Butterfly
rimane immobile, rigida come una
statua.)

ATTO TERZO

Passa la notte angosciosa. — Dal porto
al basso della collina salgono voci
confuse di marinai e rumori diversi.
— All'alzarsi del sipario è già l'alba:
Butterfly spia sempre al di fuori.

SUZUKI
(svegliandosi di soprassalto)

Già il sole! . . .

(si alza e batte dolcemente sulla spalla
a Butterfly)

Cio-Cio-San . . .

BUTTERFLY
(si scuote e fidente dice:)

Verrà, vedrai.
(vede il bimbo addormentato e lo prende sulle braccia)

SUZUKI

Salite a riposare, affranta siete . . .
Al suo venire
vi chiamerò.

BUTTERFLY
(to Suzuki)
Please come and help me dress.
No! first bring me the boy here.
(Suzuki goes to the room at the left and
brings the child and seats him near
Butterfly, who meanwhile gazes at
herself in a little mirror and says
sadly):
I'm not the same girl!
Too many sighs
have escaped from my lips,
my eyes have stared too long
at the void of the ocean.
Put on my face
a little bit of make-up;
(taking a brush, she applies rouge to
the child's cheeks)
a tiny bit for Sorrow,
for I'm afraid that
staying up so late
might make his dear little cheeks pale.

SUZUKI
(asking her to hold still)
Please, do not move, Cio-Cio-San,
while I'm brushing your hair.

BUTTERFLY
(smiling at the thought)
What will they say now, my uncle
Bonzo?
How they rejoiced to see my misfor-
tune!
And Yamadori,
the sighing suitor!
I fooled them all together;
I plucked them, those birds of a
feather!

SUZUKI
(has finished her toilette)
I've finished.

BUTTERFLY
Let me have my wedding obi.
Take care of Sorrow.
(While Butterfly dresses, Suzuki puts
another robe on the child, who almost disappears in its ample, light
folds.)
I want my love
to see me
the way I was that day.
(to Suzuki, who has finished dressing
the child)
May I please have a poppy in my
hair ...

(Suzuki puts a flower in Butterfly's
hair, who is pleased with it.)
That's right.
(with childish grace, she signals Suzuki
to close the shosi)
In the shosi we'll make three little holes
so that we can see, and
let's be silent like three little mice,
waiting patiently ...
(Suzuki closes the shosi at the rear.
Night continues to fall. Butterfly
leads the child towards the shosi. Butterfly makes three holes in the shosi,
a high one for herself, a lower one
for Suzuki, and a third, lower still,
for the child whom she places on a
cushion, admonishing him to watch
attentively through the hole prepared
for him.)
(Night has fallen; the moon's rays il-
luminate the shosi from the outside.
Suzuki, after having carried the two
lamps near the shosi, kneels and gazes
outside; Butterfly places herself in
front of the highest opening, gazing
through it, remaining motionless and
rigid as a statue; the child, who is
between his mother and Suzuki, looks
outside, but very soon falls asleep,
falling back onto a cushion; Suzuki
also falls asleep, remaining on her
haunches. Only Butterfly still remains
erect and motionless.)

ACT III

(Butterfly, still motionless, gazes outside; the child lying on the cushion,
sleeps, as does Suzuki, huddling on
the floor.)
SUZUKI
(waking up with a start)
The sunrise!
(getting up, goes to Butterfly and taps
her on the shoulder)
Cio-Cio-San ...

BUTTERFLY
(rouses herself, she says, confidently):
He'll come!
You'll see he'll come.
(Butterfly sees the sleeping child, takes
him in her arms and goes toward the
room at the left.)

SUZUKI
Please try to get some rest,
you are exhausted,
and when he gets here
I'll call you down.

BUTTERFLY

(*cantando dolcemente s' avvia per la scaletta*)

Dormi amor mio,
dormi sul mio cor.
Tu sei con Dio
ed io col mio dolor.
A te i rai
degli astri d' or:
Bimbo mio dormi!

(*entra nella camera superiore*)

SUZUKI

(*la guarda salire e dice con gran pietà:*)

Povera Butterfly!

(*Suzuki si inginocchia innanzi al simulacro di Budda, poi va ad aprire lo shosi*)

PINKERTON E SHARPLESS

(*picchiano lievemente all' uscio d' ingresso.*)

SUZUKI

Chi sia?

(*va ad aprire e rimane grandemente sorpresa*)

Oh! . . .

SHARPLESS

(*facendole cenno di non far rumore*)

Zitta! zitta!

(*Pinkerton e Sharpless entrano cautamente in punta di piedi*)

PINKERTON

(*premurosamente a Suzuki:*)

Zitta! zitta! Non la destar.

SUZUKI

Era stanca sì tanto! Vi stette ad aspettare
tutta la notte col bimbo.

PINKERTON

Come sapea? . . .

SUZUKI

Non giunge
da tre anni una nave nel porto, che da lunge
Butterfly non ne scruti il color, la bandiera.

SHARPLESS

(*a Pinkerton*)

Ve lo dissi? . . .

SUZUKI

(*per andare*)

La chiamo . . .

PINKERTON

(*fermandola*)

Non ancora.

SUZUKI

Lo vedete, ier sera,
la stanza volle sparger di fiori.

SHARPLESS

(*commosso*)

Ve lo dissi?

PINKERTON

(*turbato*)

Che pena!

SUZUKI

(*sente rumore nel giardino, sorpresa*)

Chi c' è là fuori
nel giardino?

(*va a guardare fuori dallo shosi e con meraviglia esclama:*)

Una donna!! . . .

PINKERTON

(*la riconduce sul davanti*)

Zitta!

SUZUKI

(*agitata*)

Chi è? chi è?

SHARPLESS

Meglio dirle ogni cosa.

PINKERTON

(*imbarazzato*)

È venuta con me.

SHARPLESS

(*deliberatamente*)

È sua moglie.

SUZUKI

(*sbalordita, alza le braccia al cielo, poi si precipita in ginocchio colla faccia contro terra*)

Anime sante degli avi! . . . alla piccina
s'è spento il sol!

SHARPLESS

(*calmando Suzuki e sollevandola da terra*)

Scegliemmo quest'ora mattutina
per ritrovarti sola, Suzuki, e alla gran prova
un aiuto, un sostegno cercar con te.

BUTTERFLY
(*going up the small stairs*)
Sleep, little darling,
in your mother's care.
You rest in God's lap
and she in deep despair.
The golden stars play in your hair:
Sleep, little boy of mine!
(*enters the room at the left*)

SUZUKI
(*sadly shaking her head*)
Poor Madame Butterfly.

BUTTERFLY
Sleep, little darling,
in your mother's care.
You rest in God's lap
and she in deep despair.

SUZUKI
(*kneeling before the image of Buddha*)
Poor little Butterfly!
(*a light knock at the door*)
Who is it?
(*goes to open the rear* shosi)
Oh!

SHARPLESS
Hush!

PINKERTON
(*cautions Suzuki to be silent*)
Quiet! Quiet!
(*Pinkerton and Sharpless enter cautiously on tip-toe.*)

SHARPLESS
Quiet! Quiet!

PINKERTON
(*urgently to Suzuki*)
Don't wake her up!

SUZUKI
She was terribly tired.
She never slept a wink,
waiting here for you with the baby.

PINKERTON
How did she know?

SUZUKI
Whenever these three years
any ship came to dock here,
you would find poor Butterfly
looking out for its flag and its color .

SHARPLESS
(*to Pinkerton*)
Did I tell you?

SUZUKI
(*about to leave*)
I'll call her . . .

PINKERTON
(*stopping Suzuki*)
No, not yet.

SUZUKI
You can see it:
last evening she welcomed you home
with hundreds of flowers.

SHARPLESS
(*moved*)
Did I tell you?

PINKERTON
(*disturbed*)
It hurts me!

SUZUKI
(*hears a noise in the garden, looks outside and cries out in surprise*)
Who *is* this person in the garden?
There's a lady!

PINKERTON
Steady! . . .

SUZUKI
(*agitated*)
Who can it be?

SHARPLESS
Better tell her the truth now.

SUZUKI
(*frightened*)
Who can it be?

PINKERTON
(*embarrassed*)
She has come here with me.

SUZUKI
But who is she?

SHARPLESS
(*deliberately*)
She's his wife!

SUZUKI
(*Dumbfounded, she raises her arms, then falls on her knees, her face touches the floor.*)
Ancestors sainted and holy!
Little woman,
there's no more hope,
there's no more hope!

SHARPLESS
(*calming Suzuki and helping her to rise*)
We came here so early in the morning
to talk to you alone first, Suzuki,
that in the hour of her trial
you would lend us
a helping hand.

SUZUKI
(desolata)

Che giova? Che giova?

(Sharpless prende a parte Suzuki e cerca colla preghiera e colla persuasione
di averne il consenso: Pinkerton, sempre più agitato, si aggira per la stanza ed osserva)

SHARPLESS
(a Suzuki)

Io so che alle sue pene
non ci sono conforti!
Ma del bimbo conviene
assicurar le sorti!
     La pïetosa
     che entrar non osa
     materna cura
     del bimbo avrà.

SUZUKI

E volete ch'io chieda
a una madre...

SHARPLESS
(insistendo)
Suvvia,
parla con quella pia
e conducila qui — s'anche la veda
Butterfly, non importa.
Anzi — meglio se accorta
del vero si facesse alla sua vista.
Vien, Suzuki, vien!...

SUZUKI

Oh me trista! me trista!

(spinta da Sharpless va nel giardino a
raggiungere Mistress Pinkerton)

PINKERTON

Oh! l'amara fragranza
di questi fiori
velenosa al cor mi va.
Immutata è la stanza
dei nostri amori...
ma un gel di morte vi sta.

(vede il proprio ritratto, lo osserva)

Il mio ritratto!

(lo depone)

Tre anni son passati — e noverati
n'ha i giorni e l'ore!

(agitatissimo a queste rimembranze si rivolge a Sharpless, che è ritornato a
lui vicino)

Non posso rimaner. — Sharpless,
     v' aspetto
per via.
Datele voi qualche soccorso ...

(consegna danari al Console)

Mi struggo dal rimorso.

SHARPLESS

Non ve l'avevo detto?

PINKERTON

Sì, tutto in un istante
vedo il fallo mio e sento
che di questo tormento
tregua mai non avrò.
Sempre il mite suo sembiante
con strazio atroce vedrò.
Addio fiorito asil
di letizia e d'amor.
Non reggo al tuo squallor!
Fuggo, fuggo — son vil.

SHARPLESS

Vel dissi . . . vi ricorda?
quando la man vi diede:
"Badate, ella ci crede"
e fui profeta allor!
Sorda ai consigli, sorda
ai dubbi — vilipesa
nell'ostinata attesa
raccolse il cor.
Ma ormai quel cor sincero

SUZUKI
(*desolate*)
It's useless! It's useless!

SHARPLESS

(*takes Suzuki outside and attempts to obtain her agreement, while Pinkerton becomes increasingly agitated, paces about the room and looks around*)
I know that for such sorrow
there is no consolation,
but the child awaits a tomorrow,
and we must improve his station!
See this woman
who dares not come in here?
She'll give her motherly care to him.
Come on, Suzuki, come on, Suzuki,
speak to that woman,
go and bring her in here.
If Butterfly should see her here,
it's no matter.
It might even be better if,
seeing her,
she woke up to face her future!
Come on, Suzuki,
speak to this woman.
Suzuki,
do bring her in here,
yes, bring her in here.
Come, Suzuki, please!

SUZUKI

What misfortune!
And you ask me
to tell a loving mother . . .
What misfortune!
What misfortune!
Ancestors, sainted and holy!
Poor little woman,
there's no more hope!
Oh, what heart-break!

PINKERTON

Oh! how bitter is the fragrance
of all these flowers,
like a poison to my breath.
And though nothing has changed
where once we loved
I feel the cold hand of death.
(*He notices his photograph.*)
She kept my picture.
To think three years have gone by,
three years passed since that springtime,
three long years since that springtime,
and she has counted
each passing moment.

(*Overcome by emotion and unable to retain his tears, he goes up to Sharpless and says resolutely*) :
I feel I cannot stay—
Sharpless: I'll wait for you outside . . .

SHARPLESS
Remember that I told you?

PINKERTON
Try to be kind
and help her to face it,
I know that I am guilty,
I know that I am guilty!

SHARPLESS
I told you, you remember,
Seeing that she believed you:
"Be careful.
She is in earnest."
I was a prophet then!
Deaf to all who warned her,
never doubting,
still believing
when her hopes had been deceiving,
she hoped again . . .

PINKERTON
Now, in one single moment
I see how I have wronged her,
and how this vile and craven betrayal
will be haunting my heart!

SHARPLESS
Please leave now:
the bitter truth
she had better learn alone.

PINKERTON
Farewell then, my one-time home,
filled with blossoms, and with love.
Never shall I forget her features,
hovering before me in pain.

SHARPLESS
By now, her trusting heart
can no longer be sure.

PINKERTON
Farewell now, enchanted home.

SHARPLESS
I told you,
don't you remember?
I was a prophet then!

PINKERTON
I cannot bear the thought,
Ah! how can I bear the thought!
I must flee from here.

forse presago è già.
Andate — il triste vero
da sola apprenderà.

(*Pinkerton, strette le mani al Console,
esce rapidamente, mentre Kate e Suzuki vengono dal giardino*)

KATE
(*a Suzuki*)

Glielo dirai?

SUZUKI

Prometto.

KATE

E le darai consiglio
d' affidarmi? . . .

SUZUKI

Prometto.

KATE

Lo terrò come un figlio.

SUZUKI

Vi credo. Ma bisogna ch'io le sia sola
    accanto . . .
nella grande ora . . . sola! Piangerà
    tanto tanto!

BUTTERFLY
(*dall'interno della camera superiore*)

Suzuki, dove sei?

(*appare in cima alla scaletta*)

Suzuki! . . .

SUZUKI
(*fa cenno agli altri di tacere, poi
risponde:*)

Son qui . . . pregavo e rimettevo a
    posto . . .

(*Butterfly scende: Suzuki si precipita
verso la scaletta per impedire a Butterfly di scendere*)

No . . . no . . . non scendete . . .

BUTTERFLY

(*discende precipitosa, svincolandosi da
Suzuki che cerca invano di trattener-
la, poi si aggira per la stanza con
grande agitazione, ma giubilante*)

È qui . . . dov'è nascosto?

(*vede Sharpless*)

Ecco il Console . . . e . . . dove?
    dove? . . .

(*cerca dietro ai paraventi*)

Non c'è.

(*si volge e vede Madama Pinkerton*)

Quella donna? Che vuol da me?
Niuno parla! . . . Perchè piangete?
No: non ditemi nulla . . . nulla —
    forse potrei
cader morta sull'attimo. — Tu Suzuki
    che sei
tanto buona — non piangere! — e mi
    vuoi tanto bene
un Sì, un No, dì piano . . . Vive?

SUZUKI

Sì.

BUTTERFLY

Ma non viene più.
Te l'han detto! . . .

(*irritata al silenzio di Suzuki*)

Vespa! Voglio che tu risponda.

SUZUKI

Mai più.

BUTTERFLY

Ma è giunto ieri?

SUZUKI

Sì.

BUTTERFLY
(*guarda Kate, quasi affascinata*)

Quella donna
mi fa tanta paura, tanta paura!

SHARPLESS

È la causa innocente d' ogni vostra
    sciagura.
Perdonatele.

BUTTERFLY

Ah! è sua moglie!
Tutto è morto per me!
Tutto è finito!

I must flee!
Farewell now,
I am guilty: I broke your heart . . .
Ah! forgive!

(*Shaking hands with the Consul, he exits rapidly toward the rear: Sharpless sadly shakes his head.*)

SHARPLESS

Now leave,
the bitter truth she must learn alone.

KATE
(*to Suzuki*)

And you will tell her?

SUZUKI

I promise.

KATE

You also will advise her
to entrust me . . .

SUZUKI

I promise.

KATE

I shall be like a mother.

SUZUKI

I trust you.
But you must leave me here alone beside her.
In this hour of trial leave us!
She will cry till her heart breaks,
until her heart breaks!

BUTTERFLY
(*far away, from the room at the left*)

Suzuki! Suzuki!
But where are you?
Suzuki!

(*appears at the half-closed door; Kate in order to remain unseen goes into the garden.*)

SUZUKI

I'm here.
I prayed first
and put the room in order.

(*Suzuki rushes to prevent Butterfly from entering*)

No . . no . . no . . no!
do not come down yet! No! No!

(*Butterfly enters hurriedly, freeing herself from Suzuki who tries vainly to detain her.*)

BUTTERFLY
(*moving about the room in great excitement, jubilantly*)

He's here . . . he's here . . .

Where is he hiding?
He's here . . . he's here . . .

(*discovering Sharpless*)

and the Consul, too.
Where is he? Where?

(*After having looked everywhere, in every corner, in the little alcove and behind the screen, she stares in fear.*)

Not here! . . .

(*She sees Kate in the garden*)

Who's that lady?
What does she want?
Won't you tell me!
Why are you crying?
No, no,
please tell me nothing . . .
nothing . . .
Else I might die at the moment
you spoke to me.
You, Suzuki,
so kind, and so friendly,
no, do not cry!
You who love me so dearly,
a "yes," a "no," speak softly.
Is he alive?

SUZUKI

Yes.

BUTTERFLY

But he won't return?
They have told you!

(*irritated by Suzuki's silence*)

Viper!
Answer me when I ask you!

SUZUKI

It's true.

BUTTERFLY

And yet he's back here?

SUZUKI

Yes.

BUTTERFLY

(*looks at Kate, almost fascinated.*)

Ah! how this woman
makes me tremble with anguish!

SHARPLESS

She's the innocent cause
of all your sorrow and suffering.
Do forgive her, though.

BUTTERFLY

Ah! She's his wife!
All the lights have gone out!
My life is ended! Ah!

SHARPLESS

Coraggio!

BUTTERFLY

Voglion prendermi tutto! il figlio mio.

SHARPLESS

Fatelo pel suo bene, il sacrifizio.

BUTTERFLY

Ah! triste madre!
Abbandonar mio figlio!
E sia! A lui devo obbedir!

KATE

(dolcemente)

Potete perdonarmi, Butterfly?

BUTTERFLY

(con aria grave)

Sotto il gran ponte del cielo
non v' è donna di voi più felice.
Siatelo sempre,
non v'attristate per me.

KATE

(avviandosi, dice a Sharpless:)

Povera piccina!

SHARPLESS

(assai commosso)

É un' immensa pietà!

KATE

(sottovoce a Sharpless)

E il figlio lo darà?

BUTTERFLY

(che ha udito)

A lui lo potrò dare
se lo verrà a cercare.
Fra mezz' ora salite la collina.

(Suzuki accompagna Kate e Sharpless
che escono dalla porta di destra. Butterfly si reggea stento: Suzuki si affretta a sorreggerla)

SUZUKI

(mettendo una mano sul cuore a
Butterfly)

Come una mosca prigioniera
l' ali batte il piccolo cuor!

BUTTERFLY

(si è riavuta e vedendo che è giorno
fatto si scioglie di Suzuki dicendole:)

Troppo luce è di fuor,
e troppa primavera.
Chiudi.

(Suzuki chiude porte e tende: la camera
rimane quasi in completa oscurità)

(a Suzuki)

Il bimbo ove sia?

SUZUKI

Giuoca. Lo chiamo?

BUTTERFLY

Lascialo giuocar.

(congedandola)

Va a fargli compagnia.

SUZUKI

(piangendo)

Resto con voi.

BUTTERFLY

(risolutamente batte le mani)

Va — va. Te lo comando.

(fa alzare Suzuki e la springe fuori
dell'uscio di sinistra. — Poi Butterfly accende un lume davanti al reliquiario, si inchina e rimane immobile
assorta in doloroso pensiero: va allo
stipo, ne leva un gran velo bianco
che getta sul paravento; poi prende
il coltello, che chiuso in un astuccio
di lacca sta appeso alla parete presso
il simulacro di Budda, lo impugna e
ne bacia religiosamente la lama te-
nendola colle due mani per la punta
e per l'impugnatura: quindi legge
le parole che sono incise sulla lama:)

"Con onor muore
Chi non può serbar vita con onore."

(si appunta il coltello alla gola; s'apre
la porta di sinistra e si vede il braccio
di Suzuki che spinge i bambino verso
la madre; il bimbo entra correndo
colle manine alzate; Butterfly lascia
cadere il coltello, si precipita verso
il bambino, lo abbraccia soffocandolo
di baci.)

Tu, tu, piccolo Iddio!
Amore, amore mio,
fior di giglio e di rosa.

SHARPLESS
Don't say that!

BUTTERFLY
Must I lose all I live for?
My little darling...

SHARPLESS
Think that your selfless deed
will save his future!

BUTTERFLY
Unhappy mother,
so unhappy!
To give away my son!
I shall!
I must bow to his wish!

KATE
(kindly)
You will one day forgive me, Butterfly?

BUTTERFLY
Under the vastness of heaven
there's no woman as lucky as you are.
May you be happy!
And don't feel sorry for me.

KATE
(to Sharpless who has come near her)
Poor deluded woman!

SHARPLESS
(very moved)
It's a terrible blow!

KATE
And will we get the boy?

BUTTERFLY
(who has listened)
To him I shall entrust him,
if he will come to fetch him.
You may all come back here
in half an hour.
(Suzuki accompanies Kate and Sharpless to the door. They exit in the
rear.)

SUZUKI
(placing a hand on Butterfly's heart)
Her little heart is beating wildly,
like the wings of a bird in the net!

BUTTERFLY
(Butterfly slowly recovers; seeing the
bright daylight, she breaks away from
Suzuki and says):
Too much light there outside,
and too much smiling springtime!
Close it.
(Suzuki goes to close the shosi, leaving
/ the room in almost complete dark-
ness.)
But where is the baby?

SUZUKI
Playing ... I'll call him?

BUTTERFLY
No, just let him play,
let him have his fun.
And you go and play with him!

SUZUKI
(weeping)
Please let me stay.

BUTTERFLY
(resolutely, loudly clapping her hands)
Go! This is an order!
(helps Suzuki, who is weeping desper-
ately, to get up; she pushes her out
the doorway at the left. Butterfly
kneels in front of the image of Buddha. She remains motionless, overcome by her sorrow. Suzuki's sobs are
still audible but little by little they
fade away. Butterfly has a momen-
tary spasm. She goes to the little
cabinet and from it takes the white
veil, which she throws over the
screen, then she takes the knife which
hangs on the wall in a lacquered case
near the image of Buddha. She reli-
giously kisses the blade, holding the
knife in her hands by the tip and the
hilt. In a low voice she reads the
words that are engraved on the
knife.)
"Let him die with honor,
who can no longer stay alive
with honor."
(She points the knife sideways toward
her throat. The door at the left opens;
Suzuki's arm is seen pushing the child
toward his mother; he enters, running with his little arms raised. Butterfly drops the knife and rushes up
to the child; she embraces him and
smothers him with kisses.)
You? You? You? You? You?
You? You?
My God,
my Idol!
My love,
my only darling,
pure as lilies and roses,
(taking the child's head, pressing it close
to her)
though you must not know it;
for you alone,

Non saperlo mai
per te, per i tuoi puri
occhi, muor Butterfly
perchè tu possa andare
di là dal mare
senza che ti rimorda ai dì maturi
il materno abbandono.
O a me, sceso dal trono
dell' alto Paradiso,
guarda ben fiso, fiso
di tua madre là faccia! . . .
che te'n resti una traccia,
guarda ben!
Amore addio!

*(guarda lungamente il suo bimbo e lo
bacia ancora)*

Addio! piccolo amor!
Va. Gioca, gioca.

*(Butterfly prende il bambino, lo mette
su di una stuoia col viso voltato verso
sinistra, gli dà in mano una bande-
ruola americana ed una puppattola e
lo invita a trastullarsi mentre delicata-
mente gli benda gli occhi. Poi afferra*
*il coltello, chiude la porta di sinistra
e collo sguardo sempre fisso sul figlio,
va dietro il paravento. Si ode cadere
a terra il coltello, mentre il gran velo
bianco sparisce come tirato da una
mano invisible. Butterfly scivola a terra, mezza fuori del paravento: il velo
le circonda il collo. Con un debole
sorriso saluta colla mano il bambino
e si trascina presso di lui, avendo
ancora forza sufficientt per abbrac-
ciarlo, poi gli cade vicino. In questo
momento si ode fuori, a destra, la
voce affannosa di Pinkerton che chia-
ma ripetutamente:*

Butterfly! Butterfly!

*poi la porta di destra è violentemente
scossa ed aperta: Pinkerton e Sharpless si precipitano nella stanza, accor-
rendo presso Butterfly, che con debole
gesto indica il bambino e muore. Pinkerton si inginocchia, mentre Sharpless prende il bimbo e lo bacia singhiozzando.)*

FINE

for your lovely blue eyes
dies Butterfly,
so you may live your life
beyond the ocean,
and never once remember,
when you are grown up,
that your mother abandoned you.
(with exaltation)
To me you came from heaven,
from Paradise eternal,
look at me very closely
so you'll keep a faint remembrance
of your loving mother's features.
One more glance!
Goodbye forever!
Goodbye, my darling,
my love!
(in a weak voice)
Go.
Play,
play.

(*Butterfly takes the child and places him on a mat with his head turned to the left; she places an American flag and a doll in his hands and tells him to play while she delicately blindfolds him; then she seizes the knife and, with her gaze fixed on the child, she goes behind the screen.*)

(*The knife falls to the floor, and the great white veil disappears behind the screen.*)

(*Butterfly appears from behind the screen and wavering moves toward the child. The large white veil is around her neck; with a weak smile she waves to the child and crawls toward him, still strong enough to embrace him; then she falls beside him.*)

PINKERTON

(off-stage, crying out)

Butterfly! Butterfly! Butterfly!

(*The door at the right is opened violently; Pinkerton and Sharpless enter and rush to Butterfly who, with a feeble gesture, points to the child and dies. Pinkerton falls on his knees, while Sharpless takes the child and kisses him, sobbing.*)

THE END